I0559341

I Don't Want to Go to Heaven

Judgment Day

Wayne James Coleman

McGilligan Publishing

3707 Cypress Creek Pkwy Ste 310 #505

Houston, TX 77068

www.mcgilliganpublishing.com

Copyright © Year 2024

ISBN

Hardcover: 978-1965560-07-5

Paperback: 978-1965560-06-8

Dedication

I dedicate this book to my friend Junior Tidd, who went home to be with the Lord on July 29^{th,} 2024. Even in your sickness and death, you brought healing to my spirit. I will see you again, my friend, and all those loved ones who preceded you. This book will let your loved ones know you are praying for them.

Preface

Shortly after becoming a Christian, I carried my New Testament pocket Bible everywhere. I was a truck driver then, and whenever I stopped for lunch, I read my pocket Bible. There were many things in the Bible I did not understand, but I was eager to learn. Around the same time, doctors diagnosed my wife's aunt with terminal cancer. What kind of cancer? I cannot remember. Her cancer progressed fast, and not long after her diagnosis, Aunt Mabel was admitted to the Halifax Infirmary Hospital and seemed to fade quickly. To the best of my memory, I will tell you about my visit with Aunt Mabel.

I sat beside Aunt Mabel, momentarily praying to myself, wanting to have the right words to speak. I took out my New Testament and quietly asked Jesus to guide me to the passage of scripture to read. My memory returned to a scripture reading I heard as a kid—The 23rd Psalm. What good was that? That is in the Old Testament, and I have the New Testament. I spoke to Aunt Mabel; I didn't remember all the words to the 23rd Psalm, but I know it says The Lord is My Shepherd. He will guide every step, even in those dark steps—Aunt Mabel, Jesus will be with you and never leave you.

His trustworthiness is something I know you can rely on. Despite my prayers for your healing, it has not happened. I do not understand all this Bible stuff, but I want you to be in heaven. I know you will be if you ask Jesus. Aunt Mabel, I do not know if you can hear me. I believe you can. I will pray; all you need to do is say, Jesus, I want you to be in my heart. I finished reading John 11:25, "I am the resurrection and the life. He who believes in Me, though he may die, he shall live." I left that day, not knowing if she heard what I said. The decision was not mine to make. It was in the hands of the Savior. He was the one who rose and promised life. It was never up to me. That much I knew. On my drive home, I prayed that Aunt Mabel heard my words.

Many years have passed, and many loved ones have died since I visited Aunt Mabel. Looking back, I know God was pleased with that young man's simple faith. We often think we need the right formula and must use the correct speech, but God only wants our hearts. My heart tells me Aunt Mabel heard the words of an earnest young man who wanted her to be in heaven with Jesus. Since that age and even younger, my curiosity about heaven has grown. Heaven is a mystery.

The title of this book stems from my encounter as a young boy with the sudden death of a schoolmate. I observed my sadness and the sadness of others and decided heaven was not where I wanted to go. Now, much older and having experienced the deaths of many people, I seek to understand what the Bible says happens after death.

I wanted to see if the Bible hints at what happens after death. Logos software allows me to have many digital books at my fingertips. There are 24 systemic theology books, 44 Bible dictionary sets, many commentaries, many books on heaven, and hundreds of other related topics at my fingertips. I have fewer books through Kindle and my library from my pastoral days. Combined, I am privileged to have an excellent library. I spent hours searching through them to discover as much information as possible. I mention my library to let you know you do not need an extensive library to have a growing relationship with Jesus. The late Dr. Charles Stanely often said that God revealed something new every time he looked at God's word. None of my books can ever replace God's word. I saw things in God's word I had never seen before. I read the passages, but it was as if I saw them differently. The joy of God's word reveals its truth each time you encounter it. God's word suffices to foster growth in faith.

In your walk with God, a person encounters many people who affect you, and it is impossible to mention them all. Some I have thanked personally. There are many people I could acknowledge for their influence on my life. My wife read this and gave me her feedback, and without her, this book would not have been possible. I do not think we fully realize the impact of kindness we show upon another and its influence on an individual.

Remember that there are no small deeds, and heaven records them all.

I do not consider myself a scholar. Although I love to write, my passion lies in God's word. I intend to make this journey a Biblical account of how I viewed what happens upon death. I primarily used the New King James Version and stated what version I used when I did not. It is thrilling when philosophers or scholars from various fields express profound ideas, but I always discover that the Bible said it first. All truth comes from God.

I avoid talking about the rapture and the millennium kingdom, not because they are unnecessary, but because I saw myself getting entangled and taken away from my primary purpose. I leave those topics to others. The purpose of my presentation was to discuss what happens after death and facing the King of Kings. To achieve that purpose, I attempted to avoid all timelines. I wanted this journey simple, like the young man who talked to Aunt Mabel, who did what he did and said what he said, hoping that Aunt Mabel would be in heaven with Jesus. I desire Jesus to shine through the words in these pages, and you will see His glorious plan He wants for you. Some discussions are heart-wrenching, and I have tried my best to do so with compassion. In an age where the Bible is irrelevant, we must let it speak for itself. Heaven is a mysterious journey, but it is not one we need to walk alone, nor is it a blind walk. However, it is a journey filled with excitement waiting for us who love Jesus. The purpose of this book is that you see God's love, and apart from that, we are traveling in a circle. He wants to plant our feet on Hope.

Heavenly Father, take these simple words,
And use them to glorify your Son. In Jesus
Name, Amen.

Table of Contents

Dedication i

Preface...ii

Chapter One 1

Why Talk About Heaven...1

Three Reasons We Talk About Heaven................6

We talk about Heaven so we will not become mediocre. Life is but a brief journey:...................14

We talk about heaven because we have a death sentence waiting for us...................................23

Chapter Two 34

At Death's Door...34

ANGELS - Who Are They......................................41

Angels - What do they do?..................................46

Angels 49

Chapter Three...61

A Peek Beyond Death's Door...............................61

Unexpected Beginning...80

The Great Equalizer 90

The Apostles' Creed 99

Chapter Four 103

Is This My Home?...103

What will our bodies be like? 107

Will we remember our life on earth? 109

Are there Marriages and Families in Heaven?... 112

Chapter Five 117

A Home I Did Not Imagine 117

Judgment Seat of Christ/ The Great White Throne
Judgment 138

Judgment Seat (BEMA) of Christ 140

The Great White Throne Judgment 153

The Books are Opened 168

Chapter Six 178

Now What? 178

Epilogue: 192

Seven Questions Reflected Positively 202

Chapter One

Why Talk About Heaven

I will instruct you and teach you in the
way you should go; I will guide you with
My eye. (Ps. 32:8).

Your ears shall hear a word behind you,
saying, "This is the way, walk in it,"
Whenever you turn to the right hand or
Whenever you turn to the left. (Isa. 30:21).

Whenever I babysit my grandkids at bedtime, they always want me to tell them a story. Some stories I will take from the Bible, other times I would make a story up. I always included their name in every story, but added A-Lee at the end of their name, like Chase-A-Lee. Doing so made it different, but they would identify with the character. Whether we realize it, it is like watching movies. We put ourselves into the scene, and for a moment, we live a different life. Heaven is just a story and a story we do not want to put ourselves into. There are no heroes or life-changing events that touch the deepest depths of our hearts and emotions that make us want to go there. Heaven is a place we are not in a hurry to go. Even the words of the apostle Paul to the Philippian church astound us, "I am torn between two desires: I long to go and be with Christ, which would be far better for me. But for your sakes, it is better that I continue to live." (Phil. 1:23-24, NIV). We would want to go to heaven only by necessity, "PERHAPS," but not today.

Heaven is one of those rare topics not spoken around the dinner table. Heaven is not a conversation heard at any gatherings unless we are referring to a deceased loved one. We can watch the Grammy's or any award ceremony and listen to Thanks for this Reward. We most likely never hear that someday heaven will be my biggest reward. People go on vacations and return to tell others about beautiful sites they have seen. I know what you are thinking. I have never been to heaven, so how can I talk about a place I have never been to? Someday, I will have firsthand experience, but not yet. You may have agreed with the Roman poet, Gaius Valerius Catullus, "I lived, I was not, I was, I am not; so much for that." The German philosopher Immanuel Kant may call Catullus's words "blind faith," believing based on what? I must remain focused; that can be another topic. The Bible explicitly talks about life beyond the grave. How often have you heard a sermon about heaven? Heaven is one of those topics that remains a mystery, and it has received little attention from the reformers and later Theologians. Heaven was not a central doctrine for either Luther or Calvin.[1] I do not recall learning much about heaven while in seminary. Many people often use Paul's words in his- 2nd letter to the Corinthians to explain why we don't have to know much about heaven.

I used those very words of Paul to explain away the mystery of heaven and thus need not talk about it. Paul writes to the Corinthians (2 Cor. 12:1-6, NIV), "This boasting will do no good, but I must go on. I will reluctantly tell about visions and revelations from the Lord. I was caught up to the third Heaven fourteen years ago. Whether I was in my body or out of my body, I don't know-only God knows. Yes, only God knows whether I was in my body or outside my body. But I do not know that I was caught up to paradise and heard things so astounding that they cannot be expressed in words, things no human is allowed to tell. That thing is worth boasting about, but I am not going to do it. I will boast of only my weakness. If I wanted to boast, I would be no fool in doing so, because I would be telling the truth. But I won't do it, because I don't want anyone to give me credit beyond what they can see in my life or hear in my message, even though I received such a wonderful revelation from God."

Case closed, you may say. These words of Paul said it all. We cannot know because we may not know. That's the end of the story. Is it? Let us examine Paul's words. First, we know God permits the revelation of heaven in the Book of Revelation.

John gives us a picture of heaven. A new Jerusalem is coming down to a new earth. What is happening in Corinth that Paul says he cannot tell them? We can see Boasting from (v. 1, 5-6, 11). The Corinthians were priding themselves on outdoing one another on the visions they were having. Boasting was a means of self-adulation, and Paul wanted no part. In the previous chapter, Paul told the Corinthians that he fears they are heading down the wrong path, "...I fear, lest somehow, as the serpent deceived Eve...." (11:03). There were false teachers with eloquent speech speaking a different message. Paul defends himself, "Indeed, I consider that I am not in the least inferior to these super-apostles" (1 Cor. 11:5, ESV).

Do you hear the Sarcasm in Paul's words? We can understand why Paul is told not to share his experience of heaven. He does not boast and say look at my vision, in the body or out of the body. He did not want to elevate himself in a contest of the greatest visions. Paul speaks in the third person to avoid being elevated, like the false teachers in their visions. As one writer says about talking in the 3rd person, this is a suitable manner of discourse. He argues that using the third person in such a manner means "I may speak in what will be accepted as the most inoffensive manner."[2] Paul writes, "I know a man." Paul was careful of his words when speaking to these pride-boasting Corinthians. He wanted them to hear the message of the Gospel- Christ

4

Crucified. Paul tells them, "Your pride has forced me to boast" (2 Cor. 12:11). Because of the circumstances in Corinth, Paul could not share his experiences. Paul intended for the Corinthians not to see him as unique but to focus their attention on Christ. Paul had no problem talking about his weakness so that the power of Christ may show itself (v. 9). That was the opposite of what the Corinthians were doing. They were shining through their boasting instead of letting Christ shine through them. Therefore, Paul is not saying God does not want us to know about heaven. Prophetic visions were usually in a code.[3] Nebuchadnezzar needed an interpreter. In the Book of Revelation, John gives us code for interpreting. However, we must be careful not to see more than what scripture reveals. Others may point out that Lazarus, the brother of Mary and Martha, was dead for four days and revealed nothing about heaven. Again, doing so would have taken away the reason Jesus deliberately tarried for four days when Mary and Martha asked for help. Jesus wanted to show that He was the resurrection and the life, and to talk about heaven at this point would take away from why Jesus delayed his coming. He was the resurrection and the life.

Heaven is an important topic and needs further information, or will lead to speculations. When we do not know what lies ahead, we seek or try to avoid the topic altogether, look in the wrong places, get incorrect information, and speculate.

While on his deathbed, D. L. Moody cries out: "This is my coronation Day. Don't try to call me back." Charles Haddon Spurgeon, when facing death, implored: "Can this be death? Why, it is better than living!"[4] Heaven is a mysterious topic that needs to be explored and understood. In the verses at the beginning of this chapter, David and the prophet Isaiah emphasize the need for God's guidance and direction in our lives. Therefore, we need to examine why the topic of heaven is essential.

Three Reasons We Talk About Heaven.

1. We must talk about Heaven to Know What Lies Ahead:

Lord, make me to know my end, And
what is the measure of my days, That
I may know how frail I am. Indeed, You
have made my days as handbreadths,
And my age is as nothing before You;
Certainly every man at his best state is
but vapor. Surely every man walks about
like a shadow; Surely they busy themselves
in vain; He heaps up riches, And does not

know who will gather them. And now, Lord,
what do I wait for? My hope is in You."
(Ps. 39:47).

When the pilgrims set sail on the Mayflower on September 6, 1620, excitement and apprehension filled the air. They were journeying toward a new home in Virginia. They had a land patent waiting for them. Because of religious persecution, they fled England and headed for a new start in life. Their journey did not go as planned. Just like many plans, unforeseen forces always seem to arise. They encountered various challenges during their voyage. Rough seas and navigation difficulties were not the worst of their problems. They had cramped and unsanitary living conditions. They lacked proper food, and many—faced sickness. When they set sail, there were 102 passengers plus the crew. They estimated that between 20 to 30 passengers died during the voyage to America. Sixty-six days later, they arrived, but not in Virginia. They landed in what is now known as Plymouth, Massachusetts, on November 11, 1620. Struggles were ahead of them. Instead of a home with peace and less harshness, they encountered harsh winters and limited resources. Their lack of land authority compounded their difficulties. This adventure of the Pilgrims was a journey into the unknown. They were unprepared for the challenges that awaited them. For most people, talking about heaven is a journey into the unknown—a trip filled with mystery. Although we face many uncertainties, death remains the most uncertain. We do not want to be caught unprepared like the pilgrims. We hear little about heaven, even from the pulpit, except that it is a good place.

My first encounter with death was when I was about 7; my grandfather, Coleman, died. I recall little of my grandfather Coleman, except that he raised sheep on a farm. His home had no electricity. But I enjoyed going there because I knew no one else who had sheep, and it reminded me of the Bible story of David when he was a shepherd. It seemed strange to me that someone who lived was now gone and nowhere to be found. It was like he had just disappeared. My grandfather Coleman was gone, and his sheep had also disappeared. Would I ever see my grandfather Coleman again? That thought passed. My subsequent encounter with death was when I was about ten.

We lived in Waterville, a small village in Nova Scotia. Many friends would gather and play almost anywhere in the area. This one day, we were at a friend's home playing outside, being boys. And like every other day, we eventually went home for supper. But that day was not to be an ordinary day. It was a day we would remember. That night, one of our friends died. I can still recall going to church, and Lewis, the boy who died, was lying in a box they called a casket. How still he looked lying there, looking pale. It was him, but how strange; he seemed so lifeless. How could this be? This lifeless body could not be the friend I knew, full of energy and able to join our rowdy fun. Lewis's mother clung to Lewis's Father as she staggered down the aisle. How distraught she looked all dressed in black. My heart hurt as I wondered what happened to our friend. He was now gone. His lifeless body was there, but my friend had disappeared.

How could that be? He was so young. That was my first remembrance of a minister talking about heaven. I wondered what heaven was like. Why did he need to go there? What was Lewis doing in heaven? Could he play ball? Could Lewis run and laugh? Was he sitting on a cloud? I heard they sang in heaven, but that did not sound fun. All I understood was it was supposed to be a nice place, but perhaps a sad place because we all were unfortunate. I knew I was in no hurry to go to this mysterious place called heaven. We cannot help but wonder where our loved ones are when death rips them from us. Will we ever meet them again? Do they know what we are doing? Are they watching us? I heard they are watching. If they were watching, would they not be sad just watching and seeing all the hurt? Even the thought of endless praise and singing to God is not enjoyable. Sorry, God, that is not for me—all that singing, sitting on the clouds. Maybe being an angel would be fun. Some say we become angels. No, God, I don't think

I want to go to heaven. If I could go for a visit, that would be fun.

The words of David speak of hope; "You make known to me the path of life; In your presence there is fullness of joy; At your right hand are pleasures forevermore" (Ps. 16:11, ESV). Listen to how the NIV translates the verse: "You will show me the way of life granting me the joy of your presence and the pleasures of living with you forever." Joy, living, and not just living but the pleasure of living, sound enticing.

Many people may have the impression that heaven will be dull. Other times, during this grief, we hear fables or nice cliches like God needed him, or they were now angels watching over us. Grief brings out words, thinking they are comforting. I knew a lady who spent day after day at her daughter's grave. She placed all kinds of memorabilia on and around the headstone. She lost all hope, and sadness seemed to take over. You can hear the cry of those who have no hope. Its agony reaches the most profound depth of their being. It's a cry I wish none to experience.

Grief can be an overwhelming experience. The Rev. Robert Murphy tells a story about his bipolar mom's suicide. Listen To Robert Murphy's words, "The following year, my dad called me in from a baseball game in our front yard. He sat me down on the bed and told me that "he loved my mother too much." After he sent me back to the game, he shot himself in the backyard."[5] Bishop Pike, an Episcopalian priest, was so filled with grief by the suicide of his son. Pike sought the service of a medium. I first heard about Bishop James Pike in the seventies when I read Dr. David Hunt's Book, "The Seduction of Christianity," which fascinated me. Bishop Pike said he talked to his son. How could that be? The medium had spoken and told Bishop Pike details only he would have known. I recalled that, at that moment, when I was a young lad, I had an Ouija board. I asked questions, and it was supposed to respond, and I became convinced that it did. Many think mediums and talking about spirits are but ghost stories. Scripture speaks against such acts. Why? The apostle Paul makes it clear there is another realm. The whelm of darkness reaps chaos. Listen to Paul's words about who our true enemy is, "For we do not wrestle against flesh and blood, but against principalities, against powers, against the rulers of the darkness of this age, against spiritual hosts of wickedness in the heavenly places" (Eph. 6:12). Many people put little credence in those words of Paul; instead, they label it as hocus pocus. Scientists who study string theory suggest that other dimensions exist. Scientists like Professor Leonard Susskind from Stanford, Professor Brian Greene of Columbia, and Professor Lisa Randall of Harvard are but a few. String Theory proposes extra dimensions. However, String Theory is highly speculative. Paul says there is another realm, and we must be aware of it. More and more archaeological and scientific evidence proves what the writer of the Bible tells us. Old Testament passages speak of such spirits as demons. (Lev. 19:31; 20.6, 27; Deut. 18:11-12). Daniel, chapter 10, tells of his prayer, which was delayed by evil forces until Michael the Archangel came to his aid. Many New Testament passages speak of demons. We dismiss such things as people not being advanced in thinking. Not modern. A lot of that thinking has changed with the many books that come on the market about near-death experiences. Dr. Erwin W. Lutzer says, "To try to contact the dead is to invite fellowship with hosts of darkness, pretending to be helpful angels of light. The prophet Isaiah warned the people that consulting a medium was to turn one's back on God.[6] Besides, could not Satan try to give even unbelievers a positive experience? Paul tells us, "For these people are false apostles. They are deceitful workers who disguise themselves as apostles of Christ. But I am not surprised! Even Satan disguises himself as an angel of light. So it is no wonder his servants also disguise themselves as servants of righteousness. In the end, they will get the punishment their wicked deeds deserve" (2 Cor. 11:13-15, NLT). Isaiah said, "Someone may say to you, let's ask the medium and those who consult the spirits of the dead. With their whisperings and mutterings, they will tell us what to do. But shouldn't people seek God's word for guidance? Should the living seek guidance from the dead? Look at God's instructions and teachings! People who contradict his word are completely in the dark" (Isa. 8:19-20, NIV). In the Book of Acts, we read that when people were followers of Christ, they stopped all such practices. "And a number of those who had practiced magic brought their books together and burned them in the sight of all. And they counted the value of them and found it came to fifty thousand pieces of silver" (Acts 19:19, ESV). They discarded their practices even though there was a cost to do so.

There is a story I read some time ago. There is a movie on the same theme: Wedding Crashes. Mike and Jean prided themselves on being able to crash any wedding party. They wanted something much more significant to crash than a wedding. Many people have crashed weddings. Their next big adventure would be the biggest of all. They were going to crash the Whitehouse Correspondent dinner. Mike and Jean grinned, thinking that this annual event would be a story to tell their future children and grandchildren. They got all "glammed up" in their rented attire. They had fake credentials with a French accent. The couple bluffed their way through security even though they had no invitation. They had their pictures taken with many celebrities, including several with the vice president.

People can breach security at even the most critical event. There is one event that is crash-proof. No one will enter heaven without their name written in the Book of Life (Rev. 21:27).

We talk about Heaven so we will not become mediocre. Life is but a brief journey:

The late Carlyle Marney told a delightful story of a young wife who could no longer put up with her spoiled husband. Here is the note she pinned to his coat as she sent him back home:

Dear Mother-in-law:

Attached to this note, find your infant son. I have tried to help him grow up. But you beat me to it, and you are all he needs. So, I sent him back to you, just like I got him.

Faithfully yours,

Would-be-wife

P.S. He eats almost anything, provided it's like how you fix it![7]

Sometimes, we throw up our hands in desperation. Desperation can cause people to do all kinds of things. Seeing what lies before us can ease the pain, fear, and desperation. Others feel they will never see and hear the voice of their loved ones again, so we hope and dream that this is not so. In his book, "Revealing the Mysteries of Heaven," Dr.

David Jeremiah quotes a research poll in 2015, "72 percent of Americans believe in heaven…among religiously affiliated Americans, those numbers increase: 82 percent believe in heaven. Among evangelicals, that number rises to 88 percent."[8] Dr. Jeremiah writes, "37 percent of atheists, agnostics, and people with no identifiable religion say they believe in heaven, and 27 percent of them believe in hell."[9] How can that be that even atheists cry for heaven?

We live in a time when truth has become a causality. Those statistics suggest we want more than what is present. We are spiritual creatures. Focusing on spiritual or transcendent ideals can motivate us to pursue excellence, meaning, and purpose beyond mundane or mere existence. When considering the words of our Lord, teacher, and Savior, we see there is more to life than we can imagine. There can be something greater waiting for us. Otherwise, we have what we have and battle to get more. We will face what we face and hope it all turns out for our good, which sounds like entering the unknown. And what remains for us is pondering and regrets. What if I did? For the believer, it is to be different. David informs us in the above Psalm that hope is from God (v. 7). David declared in Psalm 37:23, "The Lord directs the steps of the godly. He delights in every detail of their lives. That declaration draws us to the understanding that applying God's ways enriches our lives now and in the future.

What is more incredible is David's words that follow from his lips, "Though they stumble, they will never fall, for the Lord holds them by the hand." David told us that God has his life in His hands. Nothing can remove him from God's care. David's words hold us fast in a world where truth can become a causality of uncertainty.

Disinformation happens through social media, news outlets, and the government. How many Christians have said, "I don't know what to believe today?" Without Christians realizing it, they have fallen into Satan's plan. C.S. Lewis eloquently warned about the causality of truth in his novel, "Screwtape Letters," published in 1942. The satirical work comprised a series of letters written by a senior demon named Screwtape to his nephew Wormwood, a junior tempter. The letters offer advice on how to lead a human (called Patient) away from God and into the temptations of Hell. Screwtape's primary duty is to teach Wormwood how to manipulate Patient's thoughts and emotions so that he questions what is true and what is false.

Perhaps even worse, Western Christians have had it good over the past few decades, especially when compared to other parts of the world. Because life for the average Westerner was plenty, heaven was not a part of their mindset. History tells us that in times of persecution, the Church grew. During times of blessing, apathy was the common thread. We see the same pattern happen to Israel in the Old Testament when things were going well for them; they paid little thought to God, who gave them all they needed. Christians in not-so-affluent countries thought more about heaven because it promised a better life. So, like Israel, it seems our nature is to become mediocre when things are good. Why think about heaven when you are relaxed and comfortable? Heaven is almost unnecessary. Is heaven our true home? What awaits us beyond death's door, and are we interested? We need to be interested in knowing where we will spend eternity and what eternity will be like.

I have noticed that over the past few years, things have changed. With wars, rumors of wars, and prices skyrocketing, worrying over what disease will come next, people are looking for hope and comfort. There is a concern, perhaps even a fear, in the air. Christians are wondering if these could be the days of Noah and the days of Lot. The average age of Canadians in 2021 is 41. The average age of baby boomers is 60-78. A combination of age and fear, wondering if there will ever be a new century, has made people think more about heaven. People have experienced enhanced fears since the COVID-19 lockdowns, which brought economic distress and fear of World War III.

It's Friday, 28th February 2020. That night, there was some freezing rain. My wife and I woke up early. We planned to drive to Lady Lake, Florida, where we rented a house for two months. We had gone to Lady Lake many times before and stayed with my sister Sharon Bower and her husband Jim, and we always had a wonderful time. This time was going to be different. Our stay was to last for two months. We lay in bed, contemplating whether we should postpone our travel plans because of my aversion to driving on icy roads. We started, and we would turn around if we felt the streets were unsafe. The roads were not bad, and we arrived three days later. Not long after we arrived, COVID-19 had its impact, and lockdowns were happening. We still enjoyed the sun and did plenty of walking. My wife ended up in the hospital with AFib, which stands for atrial fibrillation, which is a type of arrhythmia or abnormal heartbeat. I didn't know that the ambulance had to shock her heart twice. That treatment is cardioversion, which involves using electrical shocks to restore the heart's normal rhythm. The hospital staff provided excellent treatment, and they discharged her three days later.

What started as an excellent vacation was anything but a dream vacation. The Canadian government advised all travelers to return home, so by April the first, we were back on the road heading to Nova Scotia. Our two-month glorious trip turned out to be different from what we expected. The government lockdown significantly impacted 2020, and we still feel its effects today. In my country, sadly, I can say that the Canadian government jailed pastors who wanted to keep their church doors open. The Reverend Dr. James Coates of GraceLife Church in Alberta was one of those pastors. Gyms, bars, Walmarts, and Home Depot were all considered essential, but Churches were not. After being closed for several months, Dr. Coates reopened his Church, going against the government order. The authorities locked the doors, even though no cases of COVID-19 had appeared in the Church for over thirty-seven straight weeks. When Coates went to court, his lawyer argued, "And in four weeks, you have a massive rodeo that will take place on the [Calgary Stampede] grounds where you'll have tens of thousands of people from all walks of life and all locations congregating to socialize and party. And then you have the Church that poses no demonstrable risk to the public."[10] Most Church members readily obeyed their governments. Was it because they believed the government and felt it had the right, or were they afraid? It could be a combination of both. Perhaps it is easier to say nothing. Most of us do not want confrontation. Dr. Coates believed he had to obey God rather than man (Acts 5:29). If we had lived in Germany during the time of Hitler, we most likely would have supported Hitler because most Germans did, and most churches agreed, or at least sat idle. Listen to Dr. Lutzer's words, "Neither the universities nor the schools challenged him [Hitler], and only part of the church had the courage to do so."[11] Hitler ruled and came to power to make things better. Mediocrity for a Christian is not an option. We are to be on guard, diligent, and about our Lord's business.

Paul writes to the Colossians, "If then you were raised with Christ, seek those things which are above where Christ is, sitting at the right hand of God. Set your mind on the things above, not on the things on earth. For you died, and your life is hidden with Christ in God. When Christ who is our life appears, then you also will appear with Him in Glory" (1 Col. 3:1-4.). But how can you look forward to something when it is a mystery? The old saying you can be so heavenly minded that you are no earthly good is a trick, by Screwtape, as C.S. Lewis so eloquently wrote in the Screwtape Letters. Heaven is important.

Jesus said He was going to prepare a place for us. As C.S. Lewis wisely says, referring to having our minds on heaven, "It does not mean we are to leave the present world as it is. If you read history, you will find that the Christians who did most for the present world were those who thought most of the next." And he further says, the apostles all left their mark on earth precisely because their minds were occupied with heaven."[12] Are we excited about going? Perhaps a better question: Do we know if we are going to heaven? If heaven were like I once pictured, I would have said no, and I don't want to go to heaven.

The Apostle Paul told Timothy to be on guard that in the last days, this will happen, "always learning and never able to come to the knowledge of the truth." (2 Tim. 3:7). There are many Biblical truths. Someone has summed this response to this truth into three categories: Watching. 2. Warning. 3. Waiting (Preparation).

1. Watching our words and actions: That is being mindful of our speech and behavior. Here are a few scripture references:

(1). Proverbs 21:23 (NIV): "Those who guard their mouths and their tongues keep themselves from calamity."

(2). Ephesians 4:29 (NIV): "Do not let any unwholesome talk come out of your mouths, but only what helps build others up according to their needs, that it may benefit those who listen."

(3). James 1:19 (NIV): "My dear brothers and sisters, take note of this: Everyone should be quick to listen, slow to speak, and slow to become angry." What a world that would be if only we paid heed to those words.

(4). Colossians 3:17 (NIV): "And whatever you do, whether in word or deed, do it all in the name of the Lord Jesus, giving thanks to God the Father through him."

(5). Matthew 12:36-37): "But I tell you that everyone will have to give account on that day of judgment for every empty word they have spoken.

For by your words, you will be acquitted, and by your words, you will be condemned."

2. Warning: Staying vigilant for signs similar to the days of Noah and Lot, as mentioned in the Bible. (Matt. 24:37-39; LK. 17:28-30). Spiritual blindness is when people turn from the things of God (2 Cor.4:3-4).
3. Watching (Preparation): Watching is active. Biblical teachings encourage us to make Jesus the center of our lives and prepare for His return. (Matt. 24:42-44; Mk. 13:32-37; 1 Thess. 5:1-6). Heaven, however, differs significantly from what I first imagined. Scripture encourages us to watch and wait for that glorious day.

Although it is natural to slip into a mundane mindset, it is not only sometimes good to let our daily activities slip to the back of our minds, but it is healthy. In the 23rd Psalm, David instructs us when things become too much to handle. God made him lie down in green pastures. "He leads me beside the still waters." Robert Alter's "The Hebrew Bible" translates, "In grass meadows He makes me lie down, by quiet waters guides me. My life He brings back." David, as a shepherd boy, would know what his duties were. To protect, care, and feed his sheep. David uses rich imagery of a shepherd with sheep under his care. You can feel the calm and peace the Good Shepard wants us to have. Just as the sheep got nourished and refreshed, God wants us to be. We need that time to refresh so we can face tomorrow.

We talk about heaven because we have a death sentence waiting for us.

A brazen preacher told the congregation, "Someday, every member of this parish will die!" The congregation was stunned, all except one man, who laughingly said, "I don't belong to this parish."[13] According to the Associated Press and the Chicago Tribune, in one year, tragedy struck twice in one family. In 1994, doctors diagnosed Ali Pierce, the fourteen-year-old daughter of John and Anna Pierce of Massachusetts, with liver cancer. She fought the disease bravely for two years, but in November 1996, she succumbed. Her parents felt overwhelming grief. To deal with the loss, the father started running and set a goal of entering the 1998 Boston Marathon. He wanted to take pledges to support the cancer center where Ali died. On October 11, 1997, John entered a half marathon of thirteen miles. It was the longest race he had ever run at fifty-one and with a clean bill of health. John set off to reach his goal. He almost finished the race. Just ten feet short of the finish line, wearing a baseball cap that said, "In Memory of Ali Pierce," John Pierce dropped dead of a heart attack.[14] We may never know what waits for us around the corner. As much as we want to be prepared for tomorrow, it is not always possible. I know a couple who had two boys, and both died a year apart in a vehicle accident. The tragedy almost ripped them apart.

Without Christ, there is no heaven, hope, or future but despair. Death, as we may remember from the story of Genesis, was the consequence of disobedience. From that point, we died spiritually and became separated from God. Watchman Nee writes, "The spirit is that part by which we commune with God and by which alone we can apprehend and worship Him. Because it tells us of our relationship with God, the spirit is called the element of God-consciousness."[15] We no longer have that free access to commune with God. We also died physically. The moment we are born, our bodies age, and our journey to the grave begins. If it were not for God's grace, Adam and Eve, as well as us, would have died eternally.

Erwin Lutzer told the story of television actor Michael Landon as he "laid on his deathbed. He saw a "bright white light" that eased his fears and made him look forward to what awaited him on the other side. He died calmly, anticipating what he called "quite an experience." How appropriate for a man who played an angel in the television series "Highway to Heaven." "[16] In the early 80s, while in seminary, I took a course at Psychic Hospital. That summer, I encountered a lady, Jean [not her real name], who had attempted suicide for the third time. She refused to talk to anyone. I would sit by her day after day until one day, she said, "I don't want to live." When life becomes unbearable, we lose all hope and believe the best recourse is death. I knew her background was Catholic, so I asked her if she knew her pain would be over after death. What if it's not? I asked her. Should we not try to see if we can deal with it now? You know there is no coming back. Eventually, Jean and I became friends and remain friends to this day. Jean never again tried to take her life. The question of what is behind death's door is an age-old question.

The understanding we will live forever somewhere is nothing new. It has shaped society's hearts and minds since the beginning of human history. Many books recount people's experiences of getting a glimpse of death. People are interested in what happens when we die. Some are so afraid of death that they will go to all means to live, even if those means are illegal, like organ harvesting. "Global Initiative Against Transnational Organized Crime" in the illicit organ trade generates an estimated $840 million to 1.7 billion annually. Then, the cosmetic surgery industry comes into play, valued at 50 billion in 2020, and projections show continued growth. We humans do not want to die. There is within every human being a struggle to live until that struggle becomes so painful that people desire death, believing it will be better.

There are even songs about heaven, and perhaps one of the most famous, at least for the baby boomers, is John Lennon's song "Imagine." In his song, he talks about imagining no heaven or hell. The song asks us to imagine, and that is where the problem begins. To imagine a place of total peace and joy are lovely words, but the scene is our imagination. To never have a sinful thought, a harsh word, or a destructive emotion is unreal in our present state. The more we struggle, the more we realize our world, for many, can be dreadful. Joel Osteen's book, "Your Best Life Now," is unreal for most of our world. Whether he realizes it, it tells us we desire heaven. God has planted in each of us a God-conscious.

Through the cross, we can access that reality. The song says we are to live for ourselves. That is what the world is doing: living for self. This song, "Imagine," is not a song of hope. It's a song about doing as you please and expecting something good. We look at our world as anything but peaceful. (if you want to understand more about God, read my book "Who Is This God: A Journey Of Faith" 2nd Edition). Imagine is a pleasant song to listen to but also a sorrowful one. It speaks of what our sinful hearts want, doing our own thing—caring only for today. The song has a dream. No war. Only peace. Those ideals go nowhere if we do not know where to find the solution. Jesus says, "Yes, I am the gate. Those who come in through me will be saved. They will come and go freely and will find good pastures. The thief's purpose is to steal and kill and destroy.

My purpose is to give them a rich, satisfying life" (Jn. 10:9-10, NIV).

Some years back, a few of my family members, my wife, and I took a trip to Italy. I researched the places we were going to visit. Like the pilgrims, I wanted to know what lay ahead. It would most likely be my only trip to Italy, and I wanted to know where I would visit. I paused while planning our vacation and realized how much effort people put into their vacations. We work all year with the hustle and bustle of life difficulties, and we may feel we need some dream vacation to make life worth living. We want to leave behind for a moment to enter a dream, which is ok. I wondered how much effect we put into thinking about the next life.

As Dr. Erwin Lutzer points out, "When facing death, denial, anger, fear, depression, and helpless resignation of these feelings erupt in the souls of those who face death. No matter that death is common to the human race; each person must face this ultimate ignominy individually. No one can endure this moment for us. Friends and family can walk only as far as the curtain; the dying one must disappear behind the veil alone."[17] That is where heaven comes on the scene. We open the veil and try to see what is behind death's door. It is not only curiosity, but it is natural. We grasp for some clue. "In early Jewish thought, heaven was a place solely for God and the heavenly hosts. Israel did not regard heaven as a place a human would inhabit-except in extraordinary instances such as Elijah (2 Kings 2:11). They believed the dead descended to the underworld-Sheol (Gen. 37:35; 42:38; 1 Kings 13:31).[18] Eventually, Heaven emerged in Jewish thought. We see this change expressed in Qumran documents. In 1947, Muhammed edh-Dhib, a shepherd, discovered the Qumran documents in the Qumran caves. By the New Testament, a more developed understanding of heaven had come to light. Disciple Matthew talks the most about heaven (84 Times). He often contrasts Heaven and Earth. Heaven is a place to store your treasures (6:9-10). Although people still misunderstand heaven, they see it as more than just a place where birds dwell or a place of stars above. The Apostle Paul called this dwelling place of God a third Heaven (2 Cor. 12:2). Jesus gave a whole new understanding of what awaits them in heaven. He called it a home. "Don't let your hearts be troubled, Trust in God, and trust also in me. There is more than enough room in my father's home. If this were not so, would I have told you that I am going to prepare a place for you" (Jn 14:1-2, NLT). To understand heaven, we must look briefly at the two phrases, the kingdom of God/the kingdom of Heaven. Although the Gospel of Matthew more commonly uses the term "kingdom of heaven," both terms are often used interchangeably. We can understand the concept as a present reality and a future hope. Believers are to live knowing God walks with them, living under His care and rule. Jesus also promises them they will dwell with Him in a future kingdom. This heaven is a whole new dwelling place. The followers of Jesus had that promise of a home so they could face life head-on. Why? The kingdom of God is now and waits for them. Because of this present and future promise, the apostle Paul roars, "O Death, where is your sting? O Hades, where is your victory?" Even though those words seem strange, too many in Paul's err, Paul loudly proclaimed and died for them.

When we examine life, we will agree with David as he echoes the brevity of life.

It matters not how long you live; you will discover life is very brief. When attending university and taking a history course on the reformation, I often would say that everyone living now will not be alive in a hundred years. We have agreed with David—life is brief. We can feel David's heart and struggle. He remembers his life and all he has encountered. The Death of Absalom brought agony to David's heart. If you have ever lost someone loved, you can identify with David. "Then the king was deeply moved, and went up to the chamber over the gate, and wept. And as he went, he said thus: "O my Son Absalom - my Son, my Son Absalom—if only I had died in your place! O Absalom my son, my son!" (2 Sam. 18:33.). What did David do? He went to the source of hope, and so must we. This whole Psalm is David's cry unto God. David's cry was that God would lift his burdens from him so he could enjoy his remaining years. It is something about reaching old age. You have the privilege of experiencing life, but old age can bring burdens. You know that life has quickly passed by. All those memories are both good and sad. David could remember pleading with God to spare his infant son bore by his wife, Bathsheba. "…while the child was alive, I fasted and wept, for I said, "Who knows whether the Lord will be gracious to me, that the child may live." But now he is dead…I shall go to him, but he will not return to me" (2 Sam. 12:22-23, ESV). Those IFS can cause havoc in our lives. All that David had accomplished seems nothing, "Surely every man walks about like a shadow; Surely they busy themselves in vain; He heaps up riches. And now, Lord, what do I wait for? My hope is in You" (Ps. 39:6-7). Amid his pain and getting close to the end of his life, his hope is in God.

This ardent golfer named Bill got up early every morning to practice. Bill was hoping to proceed into the majors. In just two days, Bill's big day would arrive. If he did very well, his dream would come true. Bill dreamed of hearing his name announced over the speaker. "Bill Jones" proceeds to the majors! The big day finally arrived; it was the 18th hole, and Bill and his arch-rival were tied. The final putt meant everything that he longed hoped for. Bill gets up to putt, full of confidence, knowing this putt means majors. Just as he swung his club, a seagull flew overhead, squawking, and Bill missed the hole.

Immediately, Bill cries mulligan. We only have one chance at life, and there are no mulligans, so we better make the most of it. When death comes - and it will, because we are born with a death sentence hanging over our heads. It is as if there is a warrant out for us, and it is only a matter of time before we get caught. No wonder we should have questions about what is going to happen after death. You see, the most crucial decision of our lives should be where we will spend eternity. The best place to find our answers about heaven is in the Bible. There is no other book in the world that can give us the comfort. No other book that promises us hope. Satan does not want you to read the road map to heaven. He has different plans for us. Even by picking up this book, you say I want to know about heaven. I want to know where I will spend eternity. It matters not how long you live; you will discover life is very brief. Let's rip back the veil and see what awaits us as we enter a new journey. Before we do, let us seek the Lord so that He may clear our hearts and minds and journey with us.

Oh, Mighty gracious Lord,
we bow our heads before You.
We know life is brief.
We know someday we face that last enemy—
death.

We thank You, Jesus, for giving us victory.
We ask You to clear our hearts and minds so that
we can hear from You.
Let us see behind the curtain and get a glimpse of
what waits for us.
Remove our fears and uncertainties so that we may
see what Jesus offers us.
In the name of Your glorious Son, Christ Jesus, we
ask. Amen!

---

[1] Garrett, James Leo, Systematic Theology, Biblical, and Historical, and Evangelical. Vol.2, end ed. 1990.

[2] Walvoord, John F. and Zuck, Roy B, Bible Knowledge Commentary, vol 2, "2 Cornthians 12," (London: Victor Books,1983). P. 582.

[3] Evans, Craig A., and David Cook, eds. The Bible Knowledge Background Commentary Acts-Philemon 2003. P. 450.

[4] Curtis Jones, 1000 Illustrations for Preaching and Teaching, "Heaven," (Nashville, Tennessee, Broadman Press, 1986) P. 149.

[5] Murphy, Robert Rev., Life after Heaven, WorHouse, West Lafayette, IN, 2022, p.35.

[6] Lutzer, Erwin W, Heaven and the AfterLife, Moody Publisher Chicago, 2017, P.180.

[7] Curtis Jones, p.178.

[8] Jeremiah, Dr. David. Revealing the Mysteries of Heaven. Dist. By Breakfast for seven, 2020, P.12

[9] Jermiah, p.12

[10] Quinton Amundson, The Catholic Register, June 17, 2021.

[11] Lutzer, Erwin W., Hitler's Cross. Chicago: Moody Publishers, 2012, p.105.

[12] Lewis, C.S., Mere Christianity: Annotated Edition (Orginal Broadcast talks England), P. 105.0

[13] Curtis Jones, 1000 Illustration for Preaching and Teaching, "Death," (Nashville, Tennessee, Broadman Press, 1986). P. 101.

[14] Larson, Crain Brian, 750 Engaging Illustrations, Baker Pub. 1993, P.109-110.

[15] Nee, Watchman, The Spiritual Man, Christian Fellowship Publishers, Inc., New York, 2014, P. 21-21.

[16] ILutzer, Erwin W, Heaven, and the Afterlife, Moody Publisher Chicago, 2017, P176

[17] Lutzer, P. 175

[18] Barry, John D. ed., "Heaven," in The Lexham Bible Dictionary (Bellingham, Washington: Lexham Press, 2016).

Chapter Two

At Death's Door

The Lord is my shepherd; I shall not want.
He makes me to lie down in green pastures:
He leadeth me beside the still waters.
He restoreth my soul:
He leadeth me in the paths of righteousness for His
name's sake.
Yea, though I walk through the valley of the
shadow of death,
I will fear no evil: for Thou art with me;
Thy rod and Thy staff, they comfort me.
Thou preparest a table before me in the presence of
mine enemies:
Thou anointest my head with oil; my cup runneth
over.
Surely goodness and mercy shall follow me all the
days of my life:
and I will dwell in the house of the Lord forever.
(Ps. 23, KJV).

James A. Pike died in 1969. His death was dramatic. During his turbulent lifetime, this controversial person turned from the practice of law to the Christian ministry, from Roman Catholic Church to Protestantism, from bishop to a church dropout, and from alcoholism and chain-smoking to abstention. Ironically, death came to the man while he was researching a new book on the historical Jesus. Wishing to rummage through old bookstalls in Jerusalem and to walk again where Jesus walked, Dr. and Mrs. Pike had gone to the Holy Land searching for information and inspiration. They became lost while driving in the desert on a sultry August afternoon. Following the grueling experiences, Mrs. Pike finally secured help. It was too late. Her fifty-six-year-old husband was dead.

A writer for the Times reported on the irony of the fact that the Right Reverend James A. Pik, once again on the brink of something new, "should perish in the wilderness of Judean desert, looking for Jesus." Reacting to the sad story, a friend comments, "Yes, and to think he could have found Him in California!"[1]

The picture of death brings upon us all kinds of uncomfortable emotions. Joseph Addison went to Oxford in the seventeenth century and applied for admission to Magdalen College. They ushered him into a black room lit by a single candle when the college president, a gloomy Puritan, appeared, and the candidate's examination was about to begin. He thought the examination would relate to Latin, Greek, or literature. Suddenly, the college president asked, "Are you prepared for death?" Addison fled, never to return.[2] Talking about death, thinking about death, and watching movies that have death scenes all arouse emotions within us. Perhaps nothing is more challenging for each of us than watching someone we love facing death.

It's Saturday, December 31, 2022, New Year's Eve, and if you walked through our front door, you would've seen my wife and I relaxing. You would see me sitting in my recliner with my feet up. My wife is nearby, playing a game on her tablet. As you can picture, neither of us is captivated by the television. My mind shifted to Kevin. Kevin was a hardworking man who loved his wife, two grown daughters, and two young grandchildren. Kevin's family meant everything to him. I was wondering what he was doing this evening. Could I have done more? I looked at my wife and said, "I will not attend church tomorrow." She looked at me with a puzzled look but said nothing. She most likely knew something was happening in my mind, for I was sitting so quietly. I did not want to mention that I believed God wanted me to stay home. What if I was wrong? What if something else was happening in my mind that I was unaware of?

Perhaps even more ironic was that a few years back, during the COVID-19 lockdown, they canceled Christmas Eve services, and I felt heartbroken. It came unexpectedly; people could go to church as long as everyone wore masks and did not sing. I remember feeling the world was crazy, allowing fear to rule lives. Here, I stayed home from church based on a sense of "Don't Go, Wayne."

Maybe I am the crazy one. So, how could I give a reason for staying home from Church?

I mentioned Kevin "WAS" hardworking because Kevin had lung cancer, and his prognosis was not good. The last enemy, death, was calling his name. Let me step back. I am getting ahead of my story.

I have not seen Kevin for 35 years. He is much younger than me. His older brother, Jerry, was my best friend growing up. Where you see one, the other is not far behind. Like many relationships, life took us in different directions. The last enemy death had called my friend Jerry. I was not around during his last days and still feel sad about that. I wanted to be there for my friend's brother, Kevin, and how that happened was that Kevin kept in contact with my mother. When Kevin was very young, my mother often babysat him. She had sent Kevin a copy of my first book, and he wanted to talk to me. I got Kevin's address, and in October 2022, I sent him a letter, and he eventually called me. Kevin loved to talk, but because of lung cancer, speaking was challenging.

Cancer would cause him to sound hoarse and be short of breath. Kevin is the type of guy who makes it easy to talk to him. It didn't take long for us to strike up a conversation. Kevin lived a few hours from me but was to have radiation therapy at the QEII and would stay at the Lord Nelson Hotel. We arranged to meet at the hotel. I arrived with a desire to share some hope. My mind was searching for words that I may say. Before I knocked on the door, I prayed, asking God for guidance. The door opened, and Kevin's wife, Debbie, a soft-spoken lady, stood before me. Upon being invited, I made my way towards Kevin, who was sitting on a chair. Now, I could put a face to the voice who I had talked to. We talked, and before I left, we prayed. I prayed, hoping that a miracle would happen.

The 15th treatment did not help. The prognosis was not good. Some days later, I received a phone call from Kevin. His first words were, "I think I am going to take the needle." He did not want his family to see him suffer. I asked him what his wife and children thought about that. He said they did not want him to do it. Kevin and I had previously talked many times about God and what Jesus did for him. I knew Kevin believed and trusted Jesus. I told Kevin we do not always see what God may have for us. Besides, spending those last days with your family will mean everything to them. I prayed with Kevin and said we would talk again. Eventually, they admitted Kevin to the Cumberland Regional Health Care Centre in Amherst.

It was New Year's Day, and I did not attend church. My wife got dressed for church, and I started my daily devotions. I continued reading God's word, wondering what He had for me that day. It seemed strange not going to church. But I believed I was not supposed to go. I still said nothing to my wife that I felt God was telling me to stay home, for I was afraid to blame God for my feelings. Perhaps my experiences of hearing people claim God told them and knowing it was incorrect. I wanted to be sure it was God telling me to stay home. Sometime later, my phone rang. Kevin's younger brother wanted to know if I wanted to go to Amherst with him to visit Kevin. I immediately said yes, I would like to go. At that moment, I knew why I was supposed to stay home. I would have missed the phone call.

We arrived at the hospital, and while walking down the hallway, I prayed for guidance. I prayed that the Holy Spirit would guide me. "Oh, Holy Spirit, be in Kevin's room, guide my tongue, bring Glory to the Father.As soon as we entered the room, I felt different. It is difficult to explain, but I knew I was not alone. Kevin's wife sat beside him on the bed; one daughter and his brother were on the right. I was on the left with his wife and daughter. I greeted him. Kevin talked as he always did, but with difficulty because of the shortness of breath. He was alert and concerned that he had taken care of everything. His wife reassured him that everything was being taken care of. I asked him if he was in pain, and he said no. I read some scripture and prayed. I told Kevin that angels surrounded his bed, ready to take him home, and his mother would be there waiting for him. This entire scene felt like a funeral service to me. As I finished talking, there were no dry eyes.

We left for home. I continued to pray for Kevin and his family. I thanked God for allowing me to take part in Kevin's life. Two days later, Kevin peacefully went to be with the Lord. There was no suffering, and Kevin spent the remaining hours with his family and then went peacefully to sleep.

The Psalm I began this chapter with is probably the most widely remembered of all 150 recorded. It's a Psalm of assurance, and since it follows Psalm 22, it is even more fitting, as the master's words cry, "My God, My God, why have you forsaken Me" (v. 1). We enter the world helpless, and we leave relying on another. Using the sheep and Shepard allegory, David displays fully what a shepherd's duty means. Jesus, being the Good Shepherd, seeks, finds, and cares. As Jesus goes to the cross, He prays, "Father, I desire that they also whom You gave Me may be with Me where I am, that they may behold My glory..." (Jn. 17:24). The Psalmist trusts the unknown. As Spurgeon writes, "We dread the unknown far above anything that we can see; a little noise in the dark will terrify, when even great mystery and uncertainty often visible do not... here the Psalmist takes the highest form of the unknown, the aspect most terrible to man, and says, even in the midst of it, he will trust."[3] I had told Kevin that angels were around him and would take him home. It is only fitting to examine what the Bible says about angels.

ANGELS- Who Are They

The one angel everyone is most familiar with is Clarence from the movie "It's a Wonderful Life," Adapted from "Greatest Gift," written by Philip Van Doren Stern in 1939, and made into a film by Frank Capra and released in 1946. Clarence, a guardian angel, receives the assignment to assist George Bailey, played by Jimmy Stewart, who is a protagonist. Although the story is fictional, there are some truths in the film. The film portrays George as a passionate, selfless man who learns his life's value and impact on others. Through Clarence's help, George finally realizes his life's value and impact on the whole town of Bedford Falls. Clarence, an angel, appears as a messenger, which is what the word Angel means.

The Old Testament and the New Testament contain many accounts of angels. The Hebrew word (mal'akh) and Greek word (angelos) means messenger. Angels act as intermediaries between the divine realm and humanity. Looking into any Bible concordance will quickly give you many references to angels and the word messenger. Below are two from the Old and New Testament:

Old Testament:

1. Malachi 3:1: "Behold I send my messenger, and he will prepare the way before me."

2. Psalm 91:11: "For he will command his angels concerning you to guard you in all his ways."

New Testament:

1. Matthew 1:20-21: "But while he thought about these things, behold, an angel of the Lord appeared to him in a dream, saying, "Joseph, son of David, do not be afraid to take to you Mary your wife, for that which is conceived in her is of the Holy Spirit. And she will bring forth a Son, and you shall call His name Jesus, for He will save His people from their sins."

2. Luke 1:11-13: "Then an angel of the Lord appeared to him, standing on the right side of the altar of incense. And when Zacharias saw him, he was troubled, and fear fell upon him. But the angel said to him, "Do not be afraid, Zacharias, for your prayer, is heard; and your wife Elizabeth will bear you a son, and you shall call his name John."

But the angels in the Bible are more than messengers; they are also protectors. Robert J. Morgan tells the story of an angel bringing protection. When I was a student at Columbia International University, my next-door roommate was Terry Hammack, who, along with his wife, Sue, faithfully served the Lord in Africa. Terry recently told me of his friend Janet Schneidermann, who labored for over forty years in northern Nigeria. She spent many years alone in Gashua and was the only expatriate missionary within fifty miles. Janet conducted much of her ministry against the backdrop of danger, and on one occasion, Nigerian colleagues warned her to leave for a safer environment. Death threats were flying like buzzards. Janet was a practitioner of Scripture memorization, and she was committing Psalm 34:7 to heart: "The angel of the Lord encamps all around those who fear Him, and delivers them." She meditated on that verse and thought, Thank You, Lord, for your promise. Your protection is excellent enough for me, so I'm going to bed rather than leave my station.

That night, four men came from town to kill Janet. As they neared the compound, they could see a tall man dressed in white with a sword in his hand guarding the front door. They felt surprised and afraid. They withdrew, and the next day, they spied out the compound and questioned locals. Nobody knew that Janet had hired a guard. That night, they returned, and again, this big guard stopped them dead in their tracks.

They casually dropped by to see Janet the next day and asked her about her guard. "I do not have a guard," she replies.

"We saw a huge man the last two nights with a long sword in his hand."

"Oh, him!" says Janet, laughing. "He must be the angel of the Lord that God promised to send because I fear Him." The men glanced at each other and hastily exited. No one ever approached her house again.[4]

Angels are also an essential part of the church. Martin Luther says, "The acknowledgment of angels is needful in the Church…they are spiritual creatures without bodies."[5] The apostle John reaffirms what Luther said. John's message to the church. "The mystery of the seven stars which you saw in My right hand, and the seven golden lampstands: The seven stars are the angels of the seven churches, and the seven lampstands which you saw are the seven churches."

There are different hierarchies of angels:

1. Seraphim: Isaiah 6:1-3. This passage describes Isaiah's vision: In the temple, praising God. They are the ones over the Ark of the Covenant and are often associated with pure light.
2. Cherubim: Often depicted as guardians. They are associated with wisdom and guarding sacred spaces. They prevented Adam and Eve from returning to the Tree of Life. Gen. 3:24; Exodus 25:18-22; Ezekiel 10:1-22.
3. Archangels: Michael and Gabriel. Daniel 10-13-14; 8:15; I Thess. 4:16; Jude 1:9; Luke 1:26-28. I Enoch 9:1; 20:1-7 mentions other archangels.

4. Angels: various passages throughout the Bible speak of angels.

Angels have no gender, no bodies, no family ties. "Each one myriad of angels was directly and individually created by God. As such, angels have no common nature which all share, nor any common stock from which all came. There is no kinship among the angels, no bond or connection to tie them together in any familial manner. Jesus affirms this, saying that "like angels in heaven," in the resurrection state, people will "neither marry nor [be] given in marriage" (Matt 22:30). In contrast, God created two of humankind and two of each animal kind-each complete with a self-replicating genetic system—He created angels in their kind.. Therefore, without an act of direct creation, there can be no addition to the angelic host."[6] Charles Wesley writes, "Concerning their essence, or nature, they are all spirits; not material beings; not clogged with flesh and blood like us; but having bodies not gross and earthly like ours, but of a finer substance; resembling fire for flame…in the words of the Psalmist: "Who makes His angels spirits, His ministers a flame of fire?" (Ps. 104:4).[7]

That does not mean angels cannot take on bodily form, which the Bible depicts. They have one purpose: to be servants of God and bring praise to Him. God has assigned them roles and ministers to humans. "And God has never said to any of the angels, "Sit in the place of honor at my right hand until I humble your enemies, making them footstool under your feet." Therefore, angels are only servants-spirits sent to care for people who will inherit salvation." (Heb. 1:13-14, NIV). The apostle Paul says we will judge angels, "Do you not know that we shall judge angels?" (I Cor. 6:3). What that judging will look like remains a mystery, but it emphasizes God's special honor and the care He has for us.

Angels - What do they do?

We have seen angels are messengers and much more. Angels are not only messengers telling Mary that God found favor in her and that she would bear a son and his name would be called Jesus. He will be the Son of the Most High. (Lk. 1:26-33). They also brought protection to Lot and his family. "And while he [Lot] lingered, the men [angels] took hold of his hand, his wife's hand, and the hands of his two daughters, the Lord being merciful to him, and they brought him out and set him outside the city" (Gen. 19:16). It is encouraging that Abraham's prayer spared Lot and his daughters from destruction. Prayer still makes a difference, and we will not know its full impact until we are in heaven. Abraham's pleading with God exemplifies God's mercy and encouragement to pray. It is also a warning that sometimes people do not listen; Lot's daughter's husbands thought it was all a joke. Despite having every chance to live, Lot's wife disobeyed and looked back. Was her heart still back in Sodom? Lot's wife could live, but she looked back. There are many places in the Bible where angels are not only messengers but also bring judgment.

Angels have the supernatural might and power to destroy at God's command. The Old Testament gives us an account of the Assyrian king Sennacherib, who had sent a threatening letter to King Hezekiah of Judah, boasting of his military might and challenging the God of Israel. Hezekiah sought the counsel of the prophet Isaiah, who reassured him that God would protect Jerusalem from the Assyrian threat. When Hezekiah prayed, God sent an angel. At that moment, 185,000 Assyrian soldiers, who were waiting for orders to attack, met their demise and fell to their death (2 Kings 19:35). In John's vision in the Book of Revelation, chapters 8 and 9, we see angels delivering judgments as plaques on the earth. That event and many other Bible stories tell us of God's power revealed in the hands of His servants. Such stories not only tell us of God's power, but that it is deadly to be on the wrong side of God. It also warms us not to put our hope in what we have, as the Assyrian King did. Also, all leaders need to be aware and examine where their legions belong. I suggest the West's fall from grace will be because it turns from God and puts hope in itself. I suggest the West's fall will be because of turning from God and placing hope in their might. Many American presidents, including Abraham Lincoln, George Washington, and others, sought God in prayer. Do they pay lip service to God? Canadian politics do not even do that. Writers of early American colonies have said three things about the Christian beliefs the people held:

1. In times of hardship, they set aside a day for prayer. Many American presidents, including Abraham Lincoln and George Washington, sought God in prayer.
2. In times of great adversity, they would engage in a day of fasting.
3. When things turned around, they celebrated with a day of thanksgiving.

Scripture tells us that God often had to allow Israel to have what they wanted so they would return to Him. God brought blessings and judgments through his ministering servants.

Angels are in that other realm that our eyes cannot see, defending, guiding, and bringing Glory to God. Number 22:21-39 provides an example. Balak, the king of Moab, summoned Balaam, a diviner, to curse the Israelites. Perhaps, out of fear and greed, Balaam agreed to do so. On his donkey, Balaam began his journey. There were three times when the donkey stopped, interrupting Balaam's journey and causing him to strike the donkey each time. Eventually, the angel revealed himself to Balaam, warning him not to curse the Israelites. Instead, Balaam blessed them. That should be a warning today with the anti-Semitism on the rise with protestors chanting, "From the river to the sea," calling for the destruction of Israel.

The International Criminal Court even wants to bring charges for this. We should always take a step back and take a deep breath before we allow our emotions to guide our directions. Do unto others as you would have them do to you is a guiding principle that has passed all time and seasons. (Matt. 7:12; Lk. 6:31). We should also be cautious and not go against God. (Gen. 12:1-3).

Angels

Angels are in that other realm where our eyes cannot see. At other times, they appear mysterious. Sometimes angels have taken on bodily form.

1. Hebrews 1:14 - "Are they not all ministering spirits sent forth to minister for those who will inherit salvation?"
2. Luke 1:26-38 The angel Gabriel announces the birth of Jesus to Mary.
3. Genesis 19 tells us a story of Lot and the angels taking on bodily form, grabbing the hand of Lot, his wife, and his daughters to get them away from destruction.
4. Matt. 28:5-7 - "But the angel answered and said to the woman," Do not be afraid, for I know that you seek Jesus who was crucified. He is not here; for He is risen, as He said. Come, see the place where the Lord lay. And

go quickly and tell His disciples that He is risen from the dead, and indeed He is going before you into Galilee; there you will see Him, Behold, I have told you."

There are some sounds that the human ear cannot hear, but they are there. It is the same with seeing. The Bible clarifies that there is another realm beyond human perception, which occasionally manifests in various ways. The Bible says the Holy Spirit teaches us how to pray. Angels intercede in our prayers. In this passage of Daniel 10:13, an angel speaks to Daniel and explains that the "prince of the kingdom of Persia" (an evil angel is a demon or Satan) opposed him, causing a delay in delivering his message to Daniel. However, the angel Michael came to his aid, allowing him to accomplish his mission. This passage suggests the idea of angelic intervention and helps in carrying out divine tasks, including delivering messages or guidance. Paul says we Christians live by faith, and in doing so, we extend a hand of God. In doing so, we may not know it, but sometimes we may entertain angels (Heb. 13:1).

When Merle and Gloria Inniger traveled from Pakistan to America, they stopped in London for a few days, and somewhere along the way, Merle locked the doors of the rental car and lost the keys. It was Saturday afternoon, and no locksmith answered the phone.

Merle and Gloria panicked about missing their flight home. Two Christian friends came to commiserate, and the four bowed their heads and prayed for help. As they finished, they looked up as a strange man approached. He offered his keys to them. The man explained he owned a similar car and perhaps his keys would work.

Merle inserted the key into the door, but it was no match. On a hope, he walked.

Around to the trunk, and in his amazement, the car key fit perfectly, and the lid popped open. His keys were on the floor of the trunk. They had fallen earlier while he was taking something out. "Praise the Lord!" everyone shouted as Merle grabbed the keys. He turned to thank the stranger, and no one was in sight. They looked in all directions, but the man had vanished. Later, Merle asked the locksmith about the chance of the man's key fitting in his trunk. It was about one in twenty thousand. "An angel?" Merle later wondered. "I have always felt he must have been."[8]

The apostle Paul says, angels watch over us. Genesis 21 tells us angels watched over Hager in the desert and Acts 12 watched over Peter in prison. Psalm 91:11, "For He shall give His angels charge over you, to keep you in all your ways." With all the power and might of angels, we are not to pray or worship them. Paul warned the Colossians not to worship angels, "Let no one cheat you of your reward, taking delight in false humility and worship angels...."(Col. 2:18). John in the Book of Revelation sees an angel and falls to worship and is told not to do so: "Now I, John, saw and heard these things, and when I heard and saw, I fell down to worship before the feet of the angel who showed me these things. Then he said to me, "See that you do not do that. For I am your fellow servant, and of your brethren the prophets, and of those who keep the words of this book. Worship God." (Rev. 22:8-9).

I will repeat a story I tell in my previous book, "Who Is This God: A Journey of Faith." As a pastor, I got to know church members and non-members of my community. Like any community, if you are there for some time, there will be deaths. I can recall this one man whose demeanor was very soft and pleasant to be in his company. I am sure you have met people like that whose demeanor was more enjoyable than some of those in your congregation. Let's call him Albert. Albert's wife was a part of the church, but he was not. I visited Albert, and we had many conversations as I often sat there sipping over a cup of tea. Sometimes, we talked about fishing; other times, what was happening? I invited Albert to church, but he felt more comfortable not going. Being young and having much to learn, I could not get him to see the value of faith. Albert eventually ended up in the hospital with terminal cancer. I do not know about you, but perhaps it's a moment older retired people reflect. Sometimes, I reflect on how things could have been, but now I see it is the hand of God's love. You never know the little things you say the Holy Spirit can use to work in the life of another.

I often visited Albert in the hospital, read him scripture, and prayed with him. One day, he accepted Christ as his Lord. I was excited. Albert had peace. I knew Albert was getting close to the end of his life, so I told him if he ever needed me, I would be there, day or night. I left the same message with the nursing station, and were to put that message on his chart. I received a call from the hospital that Albert was getting close to death. I rushed to be by Albert's side. I arrived, sat by his side, prayed, and read the 23rd Psalm. As Albert died, I saw this light. In my mind or my sight, it did not matter. I know what I had experienced was a gift from God. God grants us many blessings for some mysterious reason, and sometimes we are told the reason; other times, it remains a mystery. In all cases, God's mercy and love always astound me. However, I eventually allowed the dark angels (demons) to convince me it was all in my mind. As I type this, my heart beats fast, and tears cloud my eyes, knowing I serve a merciful God: a God who, despite our failing, extends a hand of love. But so often, we do not see it.

Death is that fearful monster that is waiting around the corner to claim its next victim. How will we face death? As the late Professor Donald Guthrie says, "It would be incomplete to discuss the hereafter without discussing death. Undoubtedly, one's belief about the afterlife affects one's attitude to death."[9] The psychiatrist Elisabeth Kubler-Ross, in her 1969 book "On Death and Dying," has an overview of the stages of death: denial, anger, bargaining, depression, and finally, acceptance. Everyone experiences these stages differently, and neither do these stages need to be linear. Some individuals may not experience these stages. Death and dying were much different in Jesus' day. "In his day, human life was cheap, and violent death was a common occurrence. Children even played at funerals (Mt. 11:16f; Lk. 7:32), so uninhibited was the general approach to the subject."[10] Perhaps even scarier than death itself is the suffering that some face before death. The Canadian government passed Bill C-14 on June 17, 2016, allowing eligible Canadian adults to request medical assistance in dying (MAID) under certain conditions. As of 2022, there were 13,241 Maid in Canada, which accounted for a 31.2% increase over 2021. People with Mental Illness were to be given the same rights in MAID as of March 2024. Because of its lack of popularity and an upcoming election, they postponed it until 2027. Many people may think death will bring peace, but that requires faith. The 18th-century philosopher Soren Kierkegaard would call it a blind leap of faith. Some years back, while still a pastor, I was called to the hospital of a critically ill man. He had bone cancer, and he was approaching death's door. As I walked down the hall to the room of the man, I was not sure what mental state the family or the dying man would be in. I knew they would be upset, but I had not known that they did not want me to mention to the dying man he was dying. They thought if he knew, he would be distraught. They tried to hide death from him. And the one thing that is impossible to do is hide death. I told them he knew. He knows how sick he is. We want to hide death because we see its pain, and most likely, we have not dealt with the mysterious monster we call death.

I began this chapter with Psalm 23, and I can close my eyes and imagine what David must have been thinking. Now, he is older. David looks back on his journey in life. He can remember as a young boy facing Goliath (1 Sam. 17), trusting God, and becoming victorious. David remembers King Saul's jealousy as he desperately tries to kill him. (I Sam. 18-31) As a father, I can only imagine having a son like Absalon, who wanted to replace his father and become king (2 Sam. 15-18). The heart ached, but God was by David's side. David says His God corrects yet brings comfort. And in his ultimate statement, David says he will dwell in the house of the Lord. David declares God will be with him whatever time he has left. The 23rd Psalm declares David's message. David says death is but a shadow.

A dark shadow may appear quite frightening but has no power to harm us. And death, unpleasant and forbidding as it may be, cannot do any actual harm to the child of God. Henry T. Mahan writes: "...Chirst has removed the substance of death and only a shadow remains. A shadow is there but it cannot hurt or destroy."[11] More and more people are opting out of having a funeral service. Old Screwtape will use all means for people to not hear the Gospel or think less about death. Even the idea of pain and suffering makes many people declare God does not care.

Pastor and author Gordon MacDonald writes: "For the first time in my life, in my thirties, I was experiencing physical pain, a spate of migraine headaches that came close to unbearable. I worried they were caused by a brain tumor and feared I would live with pain for the rest of my life. This may sound unbelievable, but I could almost set my calendar and watch to the onset of the migraines: They came during May of every even-numbered year. They hit about one o'clock in the morning every other night for about three weeks and stopped. I had four sequences of these. I finally went to a headache specialist. Ninety percent of my patients reminds me of you," he says. They are young men, heads of organizations, or want to be heads of organizations. They're not at peace with themselves; they've got some people in their lives with whom they have unresolved relationships. He had never met me and didn't know what I did for a living, but he described me perfectly.

I knew precisely the unresolved relationships to which the doctor was referring. Throughout history, some of the greatest moments of kingdom production have come during physical pain. The question then becomes, what does God want to teach me while I'm in the theater of pain? Pain humbles us, forcing us to recognize our reliance on others and God. It reduces us to our proper size. During this dark moment, Gail and I learned to pray together ten years into our marriage. It was one way I worked through my unresolved relationships. Over the next nine months, Gail and I pursued God together in prayer in more than just a superficial way, and it changed our lives. I discovered the importance of saying to her, "I need you to pray for me," which I had not done before. Years later, when Gail and I faced the blackest of my dark moments, the discipline of prayer we had learned during my physical pain was in place. We don't know all God is doing by allowing pain in our lives, but one good thing is sure: pain leads us to prayer."[12]

David plunges head-on and talks about walking through the valley of the shadow of death. He does not avoid the subject because he has hope and says; He has hope. In addition, in Psalm 37, we read that David declared, "The steps of a man are established by the Lord, when he delights in his way; though he fall, he shall not be cast headlong, for the Lord upholds his hand"(v. 23, ESV). Our comfort comes from these verses. "A man's heart plans his way, But the Lord directs his steps." (Pr. 16:9). That is the promise that He determines our life's end. You may have so many questions about my statement that my life, as I know it, will end when My God says it is now time for me to come home. I am not saying "it will be what it will be," like some fatalism. I am discussing a relationship with the Savior, where He becomes the center. He is the center of life. When I say those words, I am not declaring I am some holier-than-thou person. I declare that despite my sinful self, I belong to the Shepherd. The Shepherd determines where I go. I follow, He leads.

The Shepherd protects, guides, and shelters me. It will be the Shepherd who takes me in. Jesus knows, and I am one of his sheep, and He is my Sheperd; therefore, I trust my Shepherd. The whole point of the 23rd Psalm is that the Lord is the Shepherd. He is my "rod," which refers to His guidance and protection. Before we look at what lies beyond death's door, I must point out that, as Dr. Alcorn declares, scripture gives us images full of hints and implications about heaven. Put them together, and these jigsaw pieces form a beautiful picture."[13] Let us prepare our hearts as we jump head first into this subject of heaven to get a picture of what is beyond death's door.

Heavenly Father, we come humbly before you.

We thank you for your Son being our good Shepherd.

We thank you that you sent Him to walk this life.

We thank you for being with us in life. We will
face the last enemy death, and we confess that
because it is a mystery, it can bring fear. You
promise us that we will not walk that path alone.
Now Father, as we try to peek behind death's door,
open our eyes that we may get a glimpse of what
awaits us. Father, by giving us a glimpse the sting
of death can be removed. We ask all of this to,
bring Glory to your Son Christ Jesus. Amen!

---

[1] Curtis Jones, p.171

[2] Curtis Jones, p. 97.

[3] Spurgeon, Charles Haddon, Psalms, Kregel Publication, Grand Rapids, MI 49501, p. 113.

[4] Morgan, Robet J, Angels: True Stories, Thomas Nelson, Nashville, Tennessee, 2011, p. 24.

[5] Hazlitt. William, Esq. Chalmers, Alexander, The Table Talk, London, MDCCLVll, P. 246.

[6] McCune, Rolland, A Systematic Theology of Bblical Christianity, Vol 1: Prolegomena and the Doctrine of Scripture, God, and Angels, Detroit Baptist Theologyical Seminary, 2009, P. 351-352.

[7] Martin, Michael R., Sermon of John Wesley, Of Good Angels, Cedar Edn Books, 2008, P. 964.

[8] Morgan, Robert J, The AngeMl Answer Book, Thomas Nelson, Nashville, Tennessee, 2015, P. 31-32.

[9] Guthrie, Donald, New Testament Theology, Inter-Varsity Press, 1981, P. 821.

[10] Guthrie, Donald, P.821.

[11] Ellsworth, Roger, Opening up Psalms, Day One Publications, Ryelands Road, Leominster, HR6 8NZ, 2006, p.49.

[12] Larson, Crain Brain, P. 384.

[13] Alcorn, Randy, Heaven, Tyndale House Publishers, 2004, P. 126.

Chapter Three

A Peek Beyond Death's Door

"Preserve me, O God, for in You I put my
trust. O my Soul, you have said to the Lord,
My goodness is nothing apart from You"
Their sorrow multiplied who hasten after
another god.... I will bless the Lord who
has given me counsel; My heart also
instructs me in the night season. I have
set the Lord always before me; because
He is at my right hand I shall not be
Moved. Therefore my heart is glad, and
My Glory rejoices; My flesh will rest in
Hope. For You will not leave my Soul
in Sheol, Nor will You allow Your Holy One
to see the corruption. You will show me the
path of life; In your presence is fullness of
joy; At your right hand are pleasures
forevermore." (Ps. 16:1-2, 4f, 7-11).

For his first sermon in a preaching class, Lawrence, an African student, chose a text describing the joys we'll share when Christ returns and we are in heaven—our heavenly home awaits us. I've been in the United States for several months, he said. I've seen the great wealth here- the fine home, cars, and clothes. I've listened to many sermons in churches. I've yet to hear one sermon about heaven. Because everyone has so much in this country, no one preaches about heaven. People here don't need it. In my country, most people have very little, so we preach on heaven all the time. We know how much we need it."[1]

Perhaps the African student is correct. We may view heaven as a downgrade. Once we die off to heaven, we go. But do we? Is it a downgrade? Of course, no one wants death to come too quickly, and we may feel that it is not the worst thing that can happen to us, especially if we suffer. There are many diseases or situations we can think of where we may desire death.

Most people do not consider talking about death's door. Many do not even want to talk about the subject of death, believing it to be morbid. Why even think about it? We cannot prevent it anyway. Should we not be prepared for this one-way travel? Death's door always seemed to be a mystery that waits. As someone has said, that is one door; when it flings open with its dark pull, you can only hope for the best.

Statistics tell us most people believe there is life beyond the grave. Only 2 out of 5 think we have one life; that is all we get. Even in that group of unbelievers, only 13% rule it out entirely. And out of that, 13% will drop even lower when it involves someone who means the world to them. It is true; we must make the most out of our life. It does not mean you need to become someone famous, thinking that will give you some immortality, and that is the best you can hope for. Your name could appear on statues, buildings, or road signs, but they can all be renamed or torn down. But even that cannot guarantee that people will remember you. Eventually, we may become one of many who have lived and died and are no longer more. A friend recently told me it would have been better not to be born. He was referring to working your whole life to accumulate more things than you need. All to lose it all. "I think it is better not to be born." Was that not what Jesus said to one of his disciples? Jesus and His disciples were in the upper room. It was going to be their last meal together. They spend three years traveling together—Jesus' teaching about the kingdom of God. Telling followers to experience this new kingdom, He must die and rise again to a new life. Not one disciple seemed to grasp what Jesus was talking about.

In the dark days of the Babylonian siege of Jerusalem, God asks Jeremiah to go out and buy a piece of real estate-complete with witnesses, a deed, and money (Jer. 32:6-15). This act appeared senseless since Judah was about to be conquered, and its people would face exile. But God reminded Jeremiah that they would experience freedom in seventy years. They would return to the land to rebuild homes and replant vineyards. Jeremiah's purchase of the land was to provide a beacon of hope during the long years of captivity.

A father, at the age of seventy-five, planted several small trees. "What an optimist," the Son thought, somewhat mockingly. The dad passed away a few years later. Now, when the Son returns to the old homestead, he has the option: He can go to the grassy cemetery on top of the hill and brood over his grave, or he can eat the fruit of his trees and reflect on a man who knew a great deal about hope.

Jesus was telling the disciples that His road would lead to hope. They did not understand. Jesus says, "...one of you will betray Me." (Matt. 26:22). Can you imagine they have been by Jesus' side for three years and heard words of betrayal? You can listen to the chatter in the room. Looking at one another as they turned their heads in astonishment, wondering what Jesus was saying. No one would do such a thing. They even argued which one was more trustworthy. Then Judas, the treasurer, asked, "Rabbi, is it I?" Here are Jesus' words, "You have said it." Was Jesus not saying, look, Judas, you know it is you? (Matt. 26:19-35). Jesus tells them, "...It would have been good for that man if he had not been born." Was Jesus not saying that the fate that waits for the betrayer is far worse than anything he can imagine?

You may say, I don't need to be famous. I want to live a meaningful life and be able to put bread on the table. It would be nice to have a little extra. What am I struggling for? Listen to what Jesus says: Don't store up treasures in heaven. Did He say that? Of course not. He says, "Do not lay up for yourselves treasures on earth, where moth and rust destroy and where thieves break in and steal; but lay for yourselves treasures in heaven, where neither moth nor rust destroys and where thieves do not break in and steal. For where your treasure is, there your heart will be also." (Matt. 6:19-21). Jesus is asking what you are living for. What matters to you? Where are your heart and mind when you go about your daily life? Judas had another purpose in mind. He thought Christ was to overthrow the Roman rule and establish a new kingdom rule. Judas thought he could force Christ's hand and did not understand the type of kingdom Christ was bringing. Christ had come to bring His spiritual kingdom to earth. In the future, heaven will come down to earth.

We all have preconceived ideas and often get ahead of God's actions. When Judas realized he was wrong, remorse overtook him, and he hung himself. He acted differently than the other disciples did. Peter, for example, thought he would face death with Christ but ended up denying Christ three times.

Peter felt remorse and repented. Judas felt remorse, perhaps even shame and guilt, and committed suicide. Where is your treasure? What drives you? Listen to the words of Solomon:

The words of the preacher, the Son of David, King in Jerusalem. "Vanity of Vanities," says the Preacher; Vanity of Vanities, all is vanity." The NIV Bible reads, Everything is Meaningless, says the teacher, completely meaningless). What profit has a man from all his labor in which he toils under the sun? One generation passes and another generation comes...." (Ecc. 1:1-4).

Being older, I can look back at life and identify with Solomon. You put your heart into things, hoping it will give you meaning. You're trying to get whatever you think you need, but you mostly end up going nowhere. That is precisely how the French writer, historian, and philosopher Voltaire felt when he told his doctor, I wish I were never born. Where did his treasure lie? As sad as Voltaire's statement is, many agree with that statement. The World Health Organization stats for 2023 say over 700,000 people die every year because of suicide. Suicide is the fourth leading cause of death among 15-29-year-olds. The link between alcohol and suicide is a well-established fact. Johnny Lee, the country-western singer, has a song entitled "Looking for Love," meaning looking in all the wrong places. Those are the words of Solomon, written between 5th and 3rd centuries BC. The authors of the Bible wrote God's word as our instruction manual. When we align our spirits with Christ, we see and experience life differently. That is what the world cannot understand.

The mistake we often make, and I have made that mistake, is that we expect things to all make sense immediately. We do not understand it's a journey. Often, the church, especially in the past, acted that if a person become a Christian, they better be on the same level as those who were Christians for forty years. The Church proclaimed they believed in the Holy Spirit's power but acted as if they had to do the Holy Spirit's work. We humans have grown in technological and medical science, but the basis for life seems ungraspable. Jesus is telling each of us we have a choice of hope that leads to life or death, that leads to despair. My friend was saying nothing matters; we all end up dead. Because of the unknown, would it not be better not to be born? Jesus told Judas that what waits for you and what you do not grasp would have been better if you had never been born. That is what the world cannot understand. Jesus says to His disciples, "What I am doing you do not understand now, but you will after this." (Jn. 13:7). They did, and we can because we have the word of God. In the same way, God has given us a glimpse into heaven.

Solomon continues through all of Ecclesiastes, trying to find meaning in life until his conclusion in the last chapter, "Remember now your Creator in the days of your youth...." And then the dust will return to God, who gave it." My youngest grandson always says when I tell him a bedtime story, "AND THEN," in the last verse, Solomon declares, And Then, moment, "For God will bring every Good work into judgment, Including every secret thing, Whether good or evil." The apostle Paul's argument to the Corinthian Church is forceful when he declares, "If in Christ we have hope in this life only we are of all people most to be pitied" (1 Cor. 15:19, ESV). Paul continues by saying that through Christ, we have hope. Then he shouts, "O Death, where is your victory? O death, where is your sting?" O Hades, where is your Victory? But thanks be to God, who gives us victory through our Lord Jesus Christ" (1 Cor. 15: 55, 57, ESV). We could declare Paul's word a shout of Glory—a proclamation of victory.

I began this chapter with verses from Psalm 16, in which David expresses his prayer for guidance and protection in life. You can feel the heart of David as he prays, "Preserve me, O God." The NIV has, "Keep me safe, O God." You can almost feel David's heart shout as he calls the Lord for help. If David was getting close to death, we are not sure, but he speaks with confidence, knowing his Soul will not be left in Sheol. In Hebrew, Sheol is the grave. David is saying Do not leave my Soul in the grave. The NIV translates it, "For you will not leave my soul among the dead." Sheol is much more than a graveyard. To understand what David says, asking God not to leave his soul in "Sheol," we must know what sheol represents.

On October 7, 2006, USA Today posted a story. Five days earlier, a tragedy happened in an Amish community in Pennsylvania. Charles Carl Roberts, a 32-year-old milkman, barricaded himself inside West Nickel Mines Amish School. After murdering five young girls and wounding six others, Roberts committed suicide. It was a dark day for the Amish community of West Nickel Mines, but it was also a dark day for Marie Roberts, the wife of the gunman, and her two young children. On the following Saturday, Marie went to her husband's funeral. She and her children watched in amazement as Amish families, half of the seventy-five mourners present, stood alongside them amid their blinding grief. Despite the horrific crimes that the man had committed against them, the Amish came to mourn Charles Carl Roberts as a husband and daddy.

Bruce Porter, a fire department chaplain who attended the service, expressed profound emotion: "It's the love, the heartfelt forgiveness they have toward the family." I broke down and cried seeing it displayed." He said Marie Roberts was also touched. "She was absolutely, deeply moved by the love shown." ABC News ran a follow-up story about how the Amish forgiveness did not end there.

They visited and helped when the media besieged the Roberts family, often stepping in front of the cameras even though they didn't like their picture taken.

Contrast that with the religious leader Jesus dealt with. They were prideful and greedy, and riches meant everything to them. The religious leaders who comforted Jesus did not show a God-like attitude. They had forgotten God's promise to Abraham and the responsibility that went with that promise. "I will make you a great nation; I will bless you And make your name great; And you shall be a blessing" (Gen. 12:2). They did not understand their role, and their teachings were misplaced. Jesus often told parables to teach that their attitude led to death. Death, then what? Before we proceed further, we need to clarify that I have already stated that the sheol and Hades have the same meaning. Sheol is the Hebrew word often found in the Old Testament, whereas Hades is Greek. The problem arises in that "the translators of the King James Version caused much confusion by translating two different Greek words (Hades and Gehenna) with a one-in-the-same English word, "hell." Hades almost always denotes the "grave" or the place of the dead." Only one New Testament passage definitely describes Hades as a place of evil and punishment of the wicked and may appropriately be translated as "hell" (Lk. 16:23). In all other instances, Hades indicates nothing more than the place of the dead."[2] "Hades is essentially a place of waiting for judgment: the righteous are refreshed with a spring of water while they await the joys of paradise."[3]

I believe at this point in our journey, it will be helpful to point out the words the Bible uses for Hell and their difference with scripture references:

1. Sheol: As previously mentioned, it is a Hebrew word that signifies the grave or place of the dead, often without a specific connotation of punishment. Genesis 37, "I will go down into the grave to my son in mourning." Psalm 16:10, "For you will not leave my soul among the dead (NIV). It appears approximately 65 times.

2. Hades is the Greek equivalent of sheol. It refers to the abode of the dead. Matt. 11:23, "And you people of Capernaum, will you be honored in heaven? No, you will go to the place of the dead." Rev. 1:18, "I am He who lives, and was dead, and behold, I am alive forevermore. Amen. And I have the keys of Hades and of Death." It appears ten times in the New Testament. What is most significant about Sheol/Hades is that the grave has no hold on Christ's followers. The apostle Peter proclaimed in Acts 2:27-31 that God would not leave his soul in Hades, quoting from David in Psalm 16:10, a prophecy fulfilled in Christ Jesus. Every believer would have a

spiritual/physical resurrected body. Many believed that Hades was a prison for the ungodly and became a paradise for the believers. 1 Peter (3:18-19, CBS). "For Christ also suffered for sins once for all, the righteous for the unrighteous, that he might bring you to God. He was put to death in the flesh but made alive by the Spirit, in which he also went and made proclamation to the spirits in prison. Who in the past were disobedient, when God patiently waited in the days of Noah while the ark was being prepared." What is important to us, as J. I. Packer tells us, is simply the fact that we can now face death knowing that when it comes, we shall not find ourselves alone. He has been there before us, and He will see us through.[4] It is helpful to mention that by the 4th century, the apostle creed had established that as a belief for the church. Jesus did not descend into Hell (Gehenna) but into Hades, a place for the disembodied. Christ's death and resurrection make it possible for humanity to be made whole.

3. Gehenna refers to a specific place. Outside Jerusalem was a valley- a garbage dump. Initially, people knew it as the Valley of Hinnom. That place was where people offered child sacrifices to the god Moloch. It was where worms gnawed, and fires

never stopped burning—a place of fiery torment associated with the final judgment and eternal punishment.[5] Matt.18:8 "And do not fear those who kill the body but cannot kill the soul. But rather fear Him who is able to destroy both soul and body in hell." Mk. 9:43-44, "If your hand causes you to sin, cut it off. It is better for you to enter life maimed, rather than having two hands, to go to hell, into the fire that shall never be quenched—where their worm does not die, And the fire is not quenched." In Mark, Jesus illustrates Gehenna's dreadfulness. When we talk about Hell in this fashion, many cannot see how a loving God can send a person to such a place. First, God does not send people there; they choose that path. A garbage dump is a place void of anything good. When God created the world, He stood back and said it was good. We come to see in scripture that all goodness comes from God. Anything worthwhile has God's print of goodness upon it. In the Garden of Eden, there was no waste, no decay; everything was valuable and worthwhile. Everything in the Garden of Eden was perfect. If you remove God, you will remove anything good, anything useful. What happens in Hell is that God is giving you exactly what you want, nothing of Him. There is no goodness. There is nothing in life that has any meaning. All joy, laughter, and relationships come from God. God is removing His very presence; when that happens, there is nothing you can consider good. That is Hell. God has removed His very presence. God does not force Himself on anyone. If you do not desire Him, you end up with what remains - garbage. Those words describe a place void of God. As bad as what can happen to us in this life, there is something far worse. Gehenna appears 12 times in the New Testament.

4. Tartarus means a place holding a prisoner—the deepest part of the pit of darkness. Tartarus appears only once, in 2 Peter 2:4. "For if God did not spare the angels who sinned but cast them down to hell [tartaroo the verb cast down neither Hades nor Gehenna something far worse. They are being held in chains for the Great White Throne judgment][6] and delivered into chains of darkness, to be reserved for judgment." This sharp reminder that Peter is giving his readers is for them to remember the days of old when God did not spare the angels. He further brings to their memory the Scriptures, telling of Noah, Sodom, and Gomorrah and what happened. Peter reminds the readers to be faithful like Noah. Hold steadfast in the

faith. Peter's message is one of rescue. In the Believers Church Bible Commentary, Erland Waltner writes it is the assurance of recuse from the midst of the cultural "furnace."[7] When I think of Peter's words, my mind rushes to our day as I listen to Pastor Gary Hamrick preach on Paul's epistle to the Romans, describing our world as "losing its figgen mind." The talk of what a woman is. Men and women use the same bathroom. Men are competing in women's sports. Although written decades earlier, Erland Waltner's words about culture furnaces apply today. I wonder what word he would use today? Perhaps Gary Hamrick's words are most fitting of a world gone mad.

I know that a follower of Christ does so with a heavy heart when discussing the above words of Gehenna and Tartarus. In our world, it is easy to be sensitized and not see the misery happening, not see the people behind those words. As we pause, we can see Peter's heavy heart as he talks about a sinful world. These words make many people uncomfortable, and they should. As a young lad, I often heard the preacher talk about hell, and perhaps too frequently. Peter does not leave us feeling hopeless. He reminds us there is hope in Christ Jesus. Our next word is a phrase.

5. The Lake of Fire. The Lake of Fire is a place of judgment for the ungodly. The Lake of Fire appears five times in The Book of Revelation. 19:20, 20:10, 14-15, 21:8. It is another description of the horrors of hell.

6. Purgatory. According to Catholic theology, a person must go to this intermediate state, a place to purge their sins. This suffering can be mitigated by offering sacrifices of mass. Indulgences also arose as an effective means of paying for your sins. Luther and the Reformers all rejected the idea of retributive punishment for believers.[8] Once begun, the system spread rapidly. Not only Popes but bishops gave indulgence. You could help build a Church, bridge, or road to gain a reward.[9] Pilgrimages to sacred places like Rome were good work and paid a price for purgatory. During our family visit to Rome, we viewed the toe of the statue of St. Peter, which showed wear because of the many kisses. The Catholic Catechism states that all who die in God's grace and friendship must undergo purification to achieve the holiness necessary to enter heaven. As Dr. Wayne Grudem points out, the Catholic Church has found support for this argument not in the canonical

Scripture but in the Apocrypha, 2 Maccabees 12:42-5.[10]

However, purgatory takes away from the saving grace of the Cross. There are many scripture references against purgatory. 1 John 1:7, "But if we walk in the light as He is in the light, we have fellowship with one another, and the blood of Jesus Christ His Son cleanses us from all sin." Hebrews 9:27, "Just as people are destined to die once and after that face judgment." Phil. 1:23, "For I am hard pressed between the two, having a desire to depart and be with Christ, which is far better." The apostle Paul makes it clear when writing to the Church in Ephesus, "For by grace you have been saved through faith, and that not of yourselves; it is the gift of God, not of works, lest anyone should boast" (Eph. 2:8-9). Christ did it all for us, and to say we need to earn our way is to rob what Christ did on the cross. It is not a gift if we have to earn it. The apostle Paul writes, "For the wages of sin is death, but the gift of God is eternal life in Christ Jesus our Lord" (Rom. 6:23). "Not by works of righteousness which we have done, but according to His mercy He saved us, thought the washing of regeneration and renewing of the Holy Spirit" (Titus 3:5). Salvation is a gift. The thief on the cross asked Jesus to remember him. Jesus tells him, "Today you shall be with me in paradise" (Lk. 23:43). We will delve into the rewards that await us later.

7. Paradise: while the Bible mentions "paradise" three times, various passages imply the concept. In the Jewish background, the understanding of paradise seemed to develop. The word Paradise means park of the garden. The most famous garden that comes to mind is the Garden of Eden. This garden held the image of being free of trouble, in which the human and divine were close.[11] In early Jewish thought, there was disagreement about where paradise was located. Some saw it on earth and others in heaven. Early Jewish thought divided Sheol/Hades into two parts. In one part, the ungodly is held for judgment; in the other, the righteous are in paradise, or Abraham's Bosom (Lk. 16:22-31).[12] The apostle Paul was unsure if he went to paradise (heaven) in his body or spirit. What scripture declares is that the righteous are at peace and comfort with the Savior. The Apostle John received a revelation and spoke to the Church at Ephesus, stating, "To the one who is victorious, I will give the right to eat from the tree of life, which is in the paradise of God." Paradise can be present as referring to where those believers who died live now, but it also has an eschatological meaning. Just keep that thought for now; we will discuss it more fully later.

Let me summarize the above words. When people died, they went to the grave, Sheol/Hades. They housed the dead in two parts, with the ungodly in one part, which served as a prison awaiting judgment, and the godly in paradise, experiencing comfort. When Christ died, he descended to Hades and proclaimed the good news. Apostle Paul writes, "He ascended what does it mean but that He also first descended into the lower parts of the earth? He who descended is also the One who ascended far above all the heavens, that He might fill all things." (Eph. 4:9-10). When the scribes and Pharisees were looking for signs, Jesus told them, "For as Jonah was three days and three nights in the belly of the great fish, so will the Son of Man be three days and three nights in the earth" (Matt. 12:40). After Christ's death and resurrection, all believers go directly to Paradise/heaven. I should point out that some theologians suggest that the godly always went directly to heaven. The argument is irrelevant, for paradise has God's presence. Paul's words to the Romans give us peace and assurance, "For I am convinced that nothing can ever separate us from God's love. Neither death nor life, neither angels nor demons, neither our fears for today nor our worries about tomorrow - not even the powers of hell can separate us from God's love. No power in the sky above or in the earth below - indeed, nothing in all creation will ever be able to separate us from the love of God that is revealed in Christ Jesus our

Lord" (Rom. 8;38-39). That should end any argument or worry. We follow with Amen!

Unexpected Beginning

With those words in mind, let's journey forward toward our goal of discovering heaven. We have described some words relating to what the Bible says about what lies behind the death door. Death, the most mysterious adventure of our end-of-life story, leaves many bewildered. Life as we knew it had ended. A new beginning awaits us.

In the movie "Ghost," the main character, Sam Wheat, played by Patrick Swayze, is killed by a supposed friend. The part I want to focus on is when the friend Willie Wheat inadvertently steps into the path of an oncoming car and gets killed. After Willie's death, dark-shadowy forces appear and drag Willie's spirit down through the earth, which leaves us with the image of demons taking him to Hell. We will examine the Bible to see if it provides evidence that our spirit is escorted upon death.

"There was a rich man who was dressed in purple and fine linen and lived in luxury every day. At his gate was laid a beggar named Lazarus, covered with sores and longing to eat what fell from the rich man's table. Even the dogs came and licked his sores.

"The time came when the beggar died and the angels carried him to Abraham's side. The rich man also died and was buried. In Hades, where he was in torment, he looked up and saw Abraham far away, with Lazarus by his side. So he called to him, 'Father Abraham, have pity on me and send Lazarus to dip the tip of his finger in water and cool my tongue, because I am in agony in this fire.'

"But Abraham replied, 'Son, remember that in your lifetime you received your good things, while Lazarus received bad things, but now he is comforted here and you are in agony. And besides all this, between us and you a great chasm has been set in place, so that those who want to go from here to you cannot, nor can anyone cross over from there to us.'

"He answered, 'Then I beg you, father, send Lazarus to my family, for I have five brothers. Let him warn them, so that they will not also come to this place of torment.'

"Abraham replied, 'They have Moses and the Prophets; let them listen to them.'

"'No, father Abraham,' he said, 'but if someone from the dead goes to them, they will repent.'

"He said to him, 'If they do not listen to Moses and the Prophets, they will not be convinced even if someone rises from the dead.

(Lk. 16:19-31)

I read a story about a Sunday school teacher who wanted to explain to the six-year-olds in her class what someone had to do to go to heaven. She asked a few questions to determine what kids believed about the subject. "If I sold my house and car, had a big garage sale, and gave all my money to the church, would that get me into heaven?" she asks. "No!" the children answered. The teacher felt encouraged. "If I cleaned the church daily, mowed the yard, and kept everything neat and tidy, would that get me into heaven?" Again, the kids all shouted, "No!" "Well, the teacher asked, how can I get to heaven?" A boy in the back row stood and shouted, "You gotta be dead!" We chuckle at the boy's reply, but there is much more to the story.

The above passage of the rich man and Lazarus is a parable. Although it is a parable, there are many insights to consider. In the context of the entire chapter, we must not see this scripture declaring that rich people go to a place of torment and poor people go to a place of comfort. We get a hint of what is happening in the previous chapter. Jesus wants us to consider our attitude towards people. In Luke's Gospel, people leveled accusations against Jesus, claiming he was a winebibber, a glutton, and associated with the wrong people (Lk. 7:34). In chapter 16, Jesus wants us to see our attitude towards material possessions. As William Hendriksen's commentary points out, nowhere in the Bible are rich people condemned for being rich.[13]

However, Jesus said that it is difficult for a rich man to get saved. It is easier for a camel to go through the eye of a needle. Jesus makes that comment in Matthew's and Luke's Gospel (LK. 18::25; Matt. 19:24). Some have seen the eye of a needle referring to a gate in the wall of Jerusalem. Wuest says, "Luke, the doctor uses the medical term for the needle used in surgical operations. It refers to the tiny eye of a sewing needle, not the gate. "It is therefore impossible for anyone whose love for wealth keeps him from trusting Jesus Christ as Savior to be saved."[14] In both Gospels, Jesus describes the impossibility of saving a rich person. Why is it so difficult for a rich person? When you are rich, you have everything. A person could feel they do not need Christ. Before becoming a follower of Christ, you must believe that you need Him. That Christ is giving you something that makes life more meaningful, and without the gift, you have no hope. In June 2006, Warren Buffet, the world's second-richest man, announced he was donating 85% of his massive $44 billion fortune to five charitable foundations. He commented: There is more than one way to get to heaven, but this is a great way."[15] While Buffet is to be commended for his tremendous generosity, no one, even the world's wealthiest people, can buy a ticket to heaven.

We know riches don't provide meaning in life. Riches do not offer a way to the Truth. Jesus said He was the Truth and the Life. Giving large donations does not mean you are a follower of Christ. Jesus often spoke against people parading the giving. God created us to fellowship with Him. Some rich people have turned to drugs and ended up committing suicide. Riches cannot fulfill the purpose for which God created us. The Pharisees had religion and riches but did not have God. Christ turns everything upright. The world turns everything upside down. Earlier in Luke's Gospel, Jesus tells a story about a rich man who builds bigger barns. He feels satisfied. He says now I can eat, drink, and have fun. What happens to him? "Fool! This night your soul will be required of you; then whose will those things be which you have provided? So is he who lays up treasures for himself and is not rich toward God" (LK.12:16-21). The disciples ask Jesus, "Who, then, can be saved?" (Matt. 19:23; Lk. 18:26). In Matthew's and Luke's accounts, Jesus tells the disciples that all things are possible with God. Because God makes everything possible, we never give up seeking and praying for all the lost.

The rich man in Lazarus's story believed that while he was alive, he needed nothing. It is also worth pointing out that no other parable mentions a person's name, Lazarus. Mentioning Lazarus makes the parable more personable and more of an actual story. The name Lazarus was a common name, so we must not confuse this Lazarus with the name of Martha and Mary's brother. While not naming the rich man (Lk. 16:19) may imply no one is ultimately more important than another. "The Greek form (lazaros) of the Hebrew Eleazar (el azar) means [whom] God has helped."[16] God has helped, meaning God's eye was on Lazarus, even if it may not seem like it is. What makes this whole parable even more striking is that the religious leaders were to represent God's mercy and grace, and they were more concerned with wealth. The Pharisees professed belief in a future life but did not see they were living lives as if there was no judgment. They were living as if this life was all that mattered. They had forgotten the warnings of the prophets.

In the story, we notice two main characters: Lazarus and the rich man. Between these two characters are a few observations:

1. We see the contrast of two men, one wretched and the other wealthy. This miserable man, Lazarus, was so needy that it took dogs to lick his wounds v. 21. We can interpret the picture of dogs licking Lazarus' wounds in two ways. One to reflect Lazarus' misery and the second to emphasize that only God's creatures cared. Luke, being a physician, believes that the licking by the dogs may have a healing effect. "These dogs licked the beggar's sores as they would have their own to clean and to ease them with their tongue."[17] Dogs did what no one else would do. The rich man, clothed in purple, was a sign of wealth, as kings would wear.

2. Both men die. Lazarus dies first, followed by the rich man v. 22. The custom for the burial of a deceased would have been different for the rich man than Lazarus. Once the rich man died, neighbors would inform others and show their respect by tearing their clothes. Grieving for the deceased would last several days. When Jesus arrived at Martha's and Mary's, friends were still there on the fourth day. A common custom would be to hire professional mourners. People would have served food to the deceased family. Wailing and hiring professional wailers was a common custom for those who could do so (Mtt. 2:17-18; MK. 5:38; Acts 9:39). The rich man had everything that money could provide. No one mourned for Lazarus, and they buried him in an unmarked grave. Things were about to change for these two deceased individuals.

3. Angels escorted Lazarus to a place of rest. You may say, this is but a parable, so how much trust can we put in that? Throughout the Bible, we can see references to God taking care of His children. As early as Genesis 5:24, "Enoch walked faithfully with God, then he was no more because God took him away." (NIV). The Psalmist declares 73:24, "You guide me with your counsel, and afterward you will take me into glory." Many references throughout the Bible reflect the belief in God's peace and rest. If God promises to be with us in life, why would He not be there in our last moments? Are angels not ministering servants? The Bible does not

tell us who escorts the rich man to Hades. It leaves us wondering how the rich man arrived in Hades (v. 22-23). However, extra-biblical literature gives hints of spiritual beings taking the ungodly to the place of punishment. The rich man finds himself punished and, wants help. The rich man's experiences intensified pain in the flames of torment. Lazarus is now in Abraham's bosom. The apostle John rested on the bosom of Jesus at the Last Supper. Lazarus is now experiencing his banquet. Scripture says someday we will banquet at the marriage supper of the Lamb.

4. Not only was Lazarus carried to a place of rest, but to Abraham's bosom (v. 22). Jesus, using the name Abraham in this parable, would strike at the heart of the religious leaders—Abraham was the father of their faith. They were living contrary to what the law and prophets taught. In Deuteronomy 15:7-11, those verses instruct the Israelites to be open-handed and generous to the poor in their land, emphasizing that there would be no poor among them if they followed God's command.

With the religious leaders' greed and showmanship, they were not living according to the heart of the Old Testament. "He who has pity on the poor lends to the Lord, and He will pay what he has given" (Proverbs 19:17). Interestingly, the beloved disciple, John, rested on the bosom of Jesus, and Lazarus rested on the bosom of Abraham, both depicting comfort and reassurance of well-being.

5. The rich man experiences misery, and Lazarus lies in comfort (v. 24). The rich man cries to Father Abraham for help, but Abraham reminds the rich man of how he lived before his death (v. 25). The parable implies that what we do with our lives matters, and judgment waits for the deceased.

We also notice that Lazarus does not speak. The parable is quiet about Lazarus's interaction with the rich man. Without reading too much into this parable, we may assume Lazarus is unaware of what the rich man is experiencing. Abraham may represent God's voice.

6. There is a separation between the rich man and Lazarus. v. 26. The rich man begs for help v. 24. Interestingly, he asks Abraham to send Lazarus to comfort him. He did not ask Abraham to come, but Lazarus. Did the rich man still see himself in a different class than Lazarus? Classes, not equal, stood in the rich man's eyes. Abraham, himself, and poor Lazarus at the bottom. Even in death, the eyes of the ungodly can see or understand no differently. He cared only for himself and did not care for others, especially those who were unimportant. If self-centeredness consumes you, it compromises your ability to see or understand differently. I always felt sad for movie stars. As strange as that sounds, many have made their god their image, especially their body image. What happens when age takes that away? As hard as they try, no one can hold back the sentence of death that God said would

happen to Adam and Eve because they chose their way and not God's way. Dietrich Bonhoeffer said silence in the face of evil is itself evil. God will not hold us guiltless. Not to speak is to speak. Not to act is to act. Just because the rich man sees does not mean that what he sees changes him. There is no change for the rich man; he sees and understands things as he always did. His circumstances did not alter how he viewed things.

7. The rich man can see Lazarus in comfort. v. 23. The rich man lifts his eyes and sees Abraham and Lazarus from a distance. There is a gap between Lazarus and the rich man that no one can cross. How tormented the rich man must have been for him to see what he could not have. The guilt and the what-ifs must have been overwhelming, perhaps not for how he lived but for what he lost.

8. The rich man has his memory. He knows Abraham, and he remembers Lazarus. How often did the rich man have an opportunity to help but did nothing? Eventually, he hardly even noticed. He became no more aware than he was of the dogs. The rich man also remembers his family and desires they see what awaits them. Abraham tells him that no one can go back. They have their warnings in scripture.

9. The rich man's sense of dread for family. v. 27. Can you imagine the torment of seeing those he loved and can do nothing? Tim Chester writes, "Our life is but a moment a breath. It's a tick of the clock. A blink of an eye. A click of the fingers. You get one

life, one chance, and there is no replay, no rewind. Don't live for the moment. Live for eternity."[18]

The Great Equalizer

For the first several years of my siblings and my life, we lived in a home without bathroom facilities. That would seem strange to many in our Western world, but it would also be unthinkable. And yet, many in parts of the world live in much worse conditions. We had plenty of food on the table and always had nice clothes. Name brands did not cross our minds. Moms putting patches on our pants were a standard part of life. Excitement filled our home on Christmas as we anticipated what was under the tree. There was no talk of a basic income. Yes, some had more than others. All of us kids played together.

There was no rich man and Lazarus scene. We all seem equal before God and man, believing that working hard will help you succeed, which is what our dad did. He came from a family that had very little. Because of a broken home, he was on his own at 15. He still felt everything was possible if he worked hard. My dad, who has now gone home to the Lord, his words still ring loud and clear, "Pull yourself up by your bootstraps, work hard." He did that and achieved. Today, society has lost most of the values of my parents' generation, which contributed to its prosperity. They felt proud to pass on their values to the next generation, making life a little easier. As the recipients, we carried those same values to the next generation.

Perhaps what we may have forgotten was to pass on; there was a lot more to life than riches. Life was more than achieving materialism and making things easier. God's word said a great deal about family, relationships, and the actual value of life. There was a good reason God gave Moses the Ten Commandments. The Bible's values are logical because God is logical. Why is that so very important? When society does not adopt God's values, it ends up building upon our sinful nature. The outcome is a society that believes it's our right to have. "I-I-I-I deserve." We get a society that wants an equal opportunity, a good thing, but an equal outcome, which undermines motivation and meritocracy by rewarding regardless of effort and contributions. One says to put God first, and doing so will create a caring society that helps one another. The other says to put the government first, and they will look after everyone. It's all about understanding human nature. One sees humanity as good and will always choose the right path when given the opportunity. The other considers humanity's nature sinful and needs redemption, and only God can put its feet in the right direction.

The Bible teaches that work is a part of God's plan for humanity. It is a way to provide for yourself and an opportunity to serve and contribute to society. The Bible condemns idleness. Work honors

God; if He is the center of life, a new foundation of value and worth takes over. The beatitudes Jesus presents in Matthew chapter 5 reflect God at the center of life. None of that is possible, apart from recognizing that we are sinners and that sinners need redemption. We live to bring glory to our creator. The apostle Paul writes to the church, "And whatever you do, do it heartily, as to the Lord and not to men, knowing that from the Lord you will receive the reward of the inheritance; for you serve the Lord Christ." (Col. 3:23-24).

What we seem to have in society today is riches matter, my feelings matter, and my rights are the most important—Me, me, me. When our god becomes self, the outcome is a society struggling against power, envy, mistrust, hatred, and Chaos reigns. I deserve more than I have. Riches give power, and power is essential. Achieving power is the goal. Look at what is happening in Ukraine. None of the leaders will admit the direction of trying to remove Putin was a mistake. Those sanctions did not work. What they accomplished was more death. No leader wants to say I made a mistake. It matters, not the Western leader or the Russian; they each point fingers. They each have their agenda, and others suffer from it. However, power itself destroys. Nations throughout history have engaged in wars to attain power. The wrong use of power brings out the worst in humankind. The first person who wanted more power was Satan. He wanted to be God. He passed that on to Adam and Eve, believing my way was best for me. Nations cannot get along; they have their power games and are struggling to up one ship on another. And power struggles continue in governments, businesses, and families, between individuals and within each individual. The sad outcome is that we are blinded and do not even recognize that we are blind. Sin blinds us. It's our fallen nature. Media often feeds our fallen nature. We have a society of drug abuse, suicide, crime, war, and destruction. What is happening is struggling against our fallen, sinful nature, and we cannot win. The only solution is the CROSS. God's ways are logical because He created us in His image for Him to be with Him. Without Him, we will always struggle in the dark.

Because of the "Fall," we all have a dark side that wants to take control. Often, it demands and fights for it. Because of what happened in the Garden of Eden, the apostle Paul says the world groans to be set free. (Rom. 8:22). And the message of the Cross is that Christ came to set us free, and someday creation will experience freedom. It matters not in what part of the world; if power is not under God's control, it will create terrible conditions. Riches give "Power," and power not under God makes it impossible for a rich person to enter heaven. Riches are not even the problem. We are the problem. To what extent will people engage in evil actions to gain money? Why? Because they believe they will be finally free. Paul writes to Timothy and says, "But those who desire to be rich fall into temptation and a snare, and into many foolish and harmful lusts which drown men in destruction. The love of money is the root of all kinds of evil" (1 Tim. 6:9-11). Jesus said you cannot serve two masters (LK. 16:13-15). Serve self or serve Jesus. The darkness in us is the problem. The Bible wants us to see that death is the great equalizer for all humans. We take no riches, no power to the grave. We enter life needing another to look after us to survive, and we die needing another to live. What scripture shouts loud and clear is that there will be an equalizer, and that equalizer is death. We relinquished everything at the grave, and who we were on earth is now in God's hand. Not only does the story of the rich man and Lazarus highlight the theme of death being the equalizer, but it runs through the entire Bible. Psalm 49 highlights the vanity of wealth. Psalm 49 points out that no one can redeem their life with money, and both the rich and the poor alike face death. Psalm 49 encourages its readers to seek wisdom and understanding about the fleeting nature of life. It urges its readers to trust in God, not riches, not what riches you think will give you, for all will end in death. God will redeem those who are faithful. "This is the way of those who are foolish, and of their posterity who approves their sayings. Like sheep they are laid in the grave; Death shall feed on them" (Ps. 49:13-14). The Psalmist finds reassurance in what will happen to him at death, as he trusts God will redeem his soul from the power of the grave and welcome him (Ps. 49:15). As the common saying is, no U-hauls are going to the grave. Listen to what the Psalms say about those rich in things but not prosperous in God. "For when he dies, he shall carry nothing away; His glory shall not descend after him. Though while he lives, he blesses himself (for me will praise you when you do well for yourself), He shall go to the generation of his fathers; They shall never see light" (Ps. 49:17-19). Psalm 49 ends, "People who have wealth but lack understanding are like the beasts that perish" (NIV).The Gospel of Luke 16 and Psalm 49 are reminders of the importance of living a life aligned with God's values. King Solomon also echoes this theme of death: waiting for all. "For what happens to the sons of men also happens to animals; one thing befalls them: as one dies, so dies the other. Surely, they all have one breath; man has no advantage over animals, for all is vanity. All go to one place: all are from the dust, and all return to dust" (Ecc. 3:19-20). This same universal fate, death, awaits everyone regardless of whether they are righteous or wicked. All must face the great equalizer. Solomon concludes, "Fear God and obey his commands, for this is everyone's duty. God will judge us for everything we do, including every secret thing, whether good or bad" (Ecc. 12:13-14, NIV).

The New Testament carries that same theme, "Just as each person is destined to die once and after that comes judgment" (Heb. 9:27). The apostle James writes, "but the rich in his humiliation, because as a flower of the field, he will pass away. For no sooner has the sun risen with a burning heat than it withers the grass; its flower falls, and its beautiful appearance perishes. So the rich man also will fade away in his pursuits" (1:10-11). Those verses are but a few that point us to be wise and consider our Creator, for we all face death, and to Him we are accountable. You may say I have no problem with riches because I was never rich and will most likely never be. Riches make us feel we don't have to rely on God. Riches can be anything that takes our hearts away from God. Sin is the root of the problem. Sin tells us we are good enough. It is sin within us that says, I do not need God. Riches itself is not the problem; it is the love of it and what it can pervert in us.

Perhaps Paul Marshall and Lela Gilbert eloquently write, "It is not sin that makes music, but it is sin that fills our songs with vanity and lust. It is not sin that makes us construct cities and towers, but it is sin that makes those towers symbols of pride and power. It is not sin that calls human beings to live and love, to make music and art, to work and create, to plant and harvest, to play and dance. But it is a sin that undercuts and perverts them all. Sin does not create things, and It has no originality, creativity, or being in itself. Sin lives off that which is good. It is a parasite, feeding greedily on the goodness of what God has made. No relationship is itself sinful, but sin corrupts every relationship. No area of life is out of God's will, but we defy God's will in every area of life. It is not sin that gives us freedom of choice. But it is sin that makes us take the wrong path."[19] That wrong path is a powerful force working in our lives, and only through the power of the Holy Spirit can we have hope and victory. The message throughout the Bible speaks about the condition of one's heart and what and who controls our hearts. The rich man's pride let him believe he had all he needed. Rudyard Kipling's Poem "Mary's Son" conveys humility, obedience, and selflessness, none of which the rich man had.

If you stop to find out what your wages will be
And how they will clothe and feed you, Willie,
my son, don't go on the Sea, For the Sea will
never need you. If you ask for the reason of
every command, And agrue with people about
you, Willie, my son, don't you go on the Land,
For the Land will do better without you. If you
Stop to consider the work you have done And
to boast what your labor is worth, dear, Angels
may come for you, Willie, my son, But you'll
never be wanted on Earth, dear.[20]

Before we close with prayer, I think it is most appropriate to recite the Apostle Creed. J. I. Packer writes, "Creed means, "belief"; many Christians of the former days used to call this Creed "the Belief," and in the second century, when it first appeared, almost as we have it now, it was called the Rule of Faith.[21] Initially, Christians used it as a baptismal confession of faith. New converts recited a simpler version of the creed to affirm their belief before baptism. The creed gradually took shape over the centuries, and by the 4th century, it developed into a more structured form. The "Apostles' Creed" reflects the belief that the apostles believed. Reciting the Apostles' Creed is a shared practice among Roman Catholics, Anglicans, Lutherans, and Reformed Christians. One line in the Apostle Creed, "the holy catholic church," has caused some confusion between Catholics and Protestants. The word "Catholic" comes from the Greek word "katholikos," which means "universal." The Apostle Creed states I believe in the holy catholic church, emphasizing all Christians' unity and universality. Although the Bible does not contain the word "trinity," it presents the understanding and theology. In the same way, the Bible presents the universality of believers. 1 Cor. 12:27; Eph. 1:22-23; Heb. 12:23; Gal. 3:28; Acts 1:8. Some churches have substituted the word holy catholic church with holy Christian Church, which I have done. Another phrase has caused an argument: "He descended into Hell." In his book, Systematic Theology 2nd edition, Dr. Wayne Grudem says, "support for the idea that Christ descended into hell has been found primarily in five passages: Acts 2:27; Romans 10:6-7; Ephesians 4:8-9; 1 Peter 4:6. Dr. Grudem argues we should drop the idea of Christ descending into hell from the creed.[22] There are differences in the argument. My view is that it matters not. What does matter? All believers can agree, and what do we agree? Christ was crucified and rose from the dead and now sits on the Father's right hand of the Father. We who believe and die are with Him! When you read The Apostles' Creed, we can see the importance of declaring what scripture declares who God is, His death for us, and His promise of everlasting life. You can view that important declaration below.

The Apostles' Creed

I believe in God, the Father Almighty,
Maker of Heaven and earth;
and in Jesus Christ, His only Son, our Lord,
Who was conceived by the Holy Spirit,
born of the Virgin Mary,
suffered under Pontius Pilate,
was crucified, dead, and buried;
He descended into hell;
the third day He rose again from the dead;
He ascended into heaven,
and sitteth on the right hand of God, the Father

Almighty;
from thence He shall come to judge the quick and
the dead.

I believe in the Holy Spirit;
the holy Christian Church;
the communion of saints;
the forgiveness of sins;
the resurrection of the body,
and the life everlasting.

Now, we have come to the close of this chapter,
and before we journey to see what our merciful God
has in store for us, let us prepare our hearts so that
God may help us get a glimpse of what lies ahead
for all believers, and perhaps we will get a glimpse
of heaven.

Heavenly Father,
we bow our heads before You in the Name of the
One who offers us life—Christ Jesus.
We thank You for never forsaking us.
We praise You that Your promises of life await us,
no matter what we may face in life.
You walk with us. Our hearts may get heavy, but
we confess that sometimes we can be distracted;
You direct our paths.
Keep our eyes focused on what is essential.

Now, Father, be with us as we continue our
journey in life.

May You give us a glimpse of what glory awaits us from Your word.
We ask all of this in the name of Christ Jesus, who offers us this gift. Amen!

---

[1] Larson, Craig Brain & Elshof, Phyllis Ten, Editors, 1001 Illustrations That Connect, Zondervan, Grand Rapids, Michigan 49530, 2008, P. 166.

[2] Carpenter, Eugene E. and Comfort, Philp W. Holman Treasury of Key Bible Words, Hell, Holman Reference, Nashville, Tennessee, 2000, P.303.

[3] Freedman, David Noel, Associate Editors, Herion Gary A., Graf, David F., Managing Editor, Beck Astrid B., The Anchor Bible Dictionary, Hades, Vol. 3, Doubleday New York, London, 10103, 1992. P.15

[4] Packer, J.I., Affirming the Apostles' Creed, Crossway Book, Wheaton, Illinois, 2002, P. 89.

[5] Robertson, Archibald Thomas, A.M., D.D., LL. D., Litt.D. Word Pictures In The New Testament Vol 1, The Gospel According to Matthew, The Gospel According to Mark, Baker Book House Gran Rapids, Michigan 49506, 1930, P. 346.

[6] Vine, W. E.; Unger, Merrill F.; White, William, Jr., The Expository Dictionary of Biblical Words, Hell, Thomas Nelson Publishers, New York, 1985, P. 300.

[7] Waltner, Erland; Charles, Daryl J., Believers Church Bible Commentary, 2 Peter, Herald Press, Scottdale, Pa. 15683, 1988, P. 236.

[8] Davie, Martin., Grass, Tim., Holmes, Stephen R. Holmes., McDowell, John., Noble, T.A., Editors, New Dictionary Of Theology, Historical and Systematic, 2nd Edition, Inter-varsity Press, 2016, Purgatory, P. 719.

[9] Walker, Walker, Revised by Handy, Robert., Richardson, Cyril C., Pauck, Wilhelm, Handy, Robert., A History Of The Christian Church, 3rd Edition, Charles Scribner's Sons, New York, 1970, P. 250.

[10] Grudem, Wayne, An Introduction to Biblical Doctrine, Systematic Theology 2nd Edition, Death and the intermediate State, Zondervan Academic, Michigan, Grand Rapids, 2020, P. 1947.

[11] Freed

[12] Buttrick, G.A., Kepler, T.S., Knox, J., May, H.G., & Terrien S. (Eds.). The Interpreter's Dictionary Of The Bible, (Vol K-Q), Paradise, Nashville, TN: Abington, P. 656.

[13] Hendriksen, William, New Testament Commentary, Exposition of the Gospel According to Luke, Baker Book House, Grand Rapids Michigan, 1981, P. 782.

[14] West, Kenneth S., Wuest's Word Studies From the Greek New Testament, Vol. 3, Eerdmans Publishing, Grand Rapids, Michigan 49502, 1952, P..29,

[15] Rhodes, Rodes, The Wonder of Heaven, Harvest House Publishers, Eugene, Oregon, 2009, P.217.

[16] Gaebelein, Frank E. The Expositor's Bible Commentary Vol 8, Matthew, Mark, Luke, Regency Reference Library, 1984, P. 981.

[17] Earle, Ralph, Word Meanings in the New Testament Vol. 1, Beacon Hill Press, Kansas City, Missouri, 1986, P. 71.

[18] Chester, Time, The Ordinary Hero: Living the Cross and the Resurrection, InterVarsity Press, Nothingham England, 2009, P. 207.

[19] Marshall, Paul; Gilbert, Lela, Heaven Is Not My Home, Word Publishing, Nashville, 1998. P. 32-33.

[20] Rudyard, Kipling, "Mary's Son," Poetry lovers' Page, accessed June 17, 2024 https://www.poetryloverspage.com

[21] Packer, J.I., Affirming the Apostles' Creed, Crossway Book, Wheaton, Illinois, 2008, P.11.

[22] Grudem, Wayne, P. 1406-7.

Chapter Four

Is This My Home?

"Don't let your hearts be troubled. Trust in God, and trust also in me. There is more than enough room in my Father's home. If this were not so, would I have told you that I am going to prepare a place for you? When everything is ready, I will come and get you, so that you always be with me where I am." (Jn. 14:1-3, NIV).

I read a story about a family of four, and I changed the story to suit my purpose—the parents were Brain and his wife, Becky. Brain and Becky had four children: two boys, Josh and Chase, ages 15 and 8, and two girls, Ava, 11, and Madalyn, 6. Since their honeymoon, Brain and Becky had never taken a vacation together. Brain's parents talked them into taking a trip together while they looked after the children. The children had never been apart from their parents, but their grandparents reassured them they would have fun, pool splashing, the park, and lots of snuggle time. So, Brain and Becky go to a wilderness cabin for hiking and leisure time, while Josh, Chase, Ava, and Madalyn look forward to spending time with their grandparents.

On day three, when the children's parents were gone, the grandmother slipped into the boys' room around 7 p.m. to give last-minute hugs and kisses, and the boys seemed to settle in quite well. The next day, it rained and seemed to go on forever. The grandparents kept the Children busy playing games and watching videos.

At last, it was time for bed; the grandparents were tired. Then the phone rang. It was Brain and Becky, and the children jumped up to chat. Madalyn, being the youngest, talked first. The tears flowed down Madalyn's cheek as she spoke to her parents. Tears, they seem to catch. The tears started flowing as Ava, Chase, and Josh talked to their parents. As much as they loved Grandma and Grandpa, they missed Mom and Dad. As much as Brain and Becky enjoyed their time together, they missed the kids.

The grandparents tried to quiet the boys. Eventually, each of the children fell asleep. Mom and Dad learned to call when the children weren't so tired during the day. Five days later, the parents returned home. Josh, Chase, Ava, and Madalyn ran to hug their parents as they entered the home. The home was complete at last.

After reading and adjusting the story, my memory of when I was a boy flashed back. My dad began a teaching position in Springhill, Nova Scotia. We had lived all my first 12 years of life next door to my grandparents. My daily routine was to pop into my grandparents' home and see my grandmother baking cookies. As I entered the door of my grandparents' house, I could smell the aroma of molasses cookies. These were no ordinary cookies; my grandmother had perfected them over the years. When he was a boy, my uncle Keith called them "Flying Saucers, O boy." They were big and tasty.

We no longer lived next door to my grandparents; not seeing them daily was difficult. Then, one day, my grandparents came to visit. What an exciting time that was for us three kids. But the sad part came when they had to leave. I can recall tears rolling down our cheeks. Why did I tell you these two stories? I want you to picture the feeling of family. I recognize some people were not fortunate to experience such a treasure, and it is sad to think they missed out on one of God's splendid gifts. No one needs to miss out on that feeling of family that Jesus says is waiting for each of us. He is gone to prepare a place for His children. This understanding of family is essential as we venture into our next journey of what Christ has prepared for us. In addition, my wife always says it's nice to be home again when we are away. I cannot count the times when we have entered our door and heard her say those words. I want us to grasp the feeling of family and home as we see what Christ has waiting for us. We are just not going to any old place. We are going home. To a place our Heavenly Father wanted us to have from the beginning.

We began this chapter with Jesus' words from the gospel of John. Let not your hearts be sad. I will go to prepare a home for you. It is this feeling of Jesus comforting His children and preparing them for Him leaving them. Jesus wants them to know that heaven is a home—the Hebrew word house, "Bayit" (house, dwelling, home, family). The Greek word house is "Oikos" (house, household, family). It means more than a house; it means to produce a family.[1] This "HOME" that we will have is for those who the apostle Paul writes, "If you confess with your mouth, Jesus is Lord, and believe in your heart that God raised him from the dead, you will be saved. One believes with the heart, resulting in righteousness, and one confesses with the mouth, resulting in salvation." (Rom. 10:9-10, CSB)

Before I tell you about the home we are going to, I am sure you have a few questions, so let me try to answer some of the obvious ones. Many questions about heaven remain unanswered, and we continue to be mystified by many others. However, I believe there are enough answers to help us feel comfortable and perhaps excited about the place we will call home.

What will our bodies be like?

Many have thought our resurrected body will only be spiritual. Perhaps we get that idea from the many ghost stories we all heard of or movies like the one by Charles Dickens - "Scrooge," where Jacob Marley appears to Ebenezer Scrooge to get him to see the path he is on will lead to pain and agony. The Old Testament has a similar story in 1 Samuel 28, where King Saul was to face the Philistine army. Because of his disobedience, he was desperate for guidance after God ceased communicating with him. Saul wanted advice from Samuel, who had died. He goes to a medium at Endor to summon the prophet Samuel. The narrative describes Samuel's appearance in a recognizable form. That is not the resurrected body Christ promised us. The resurrected body will be physical, not merely spiritual. Jesus' resurrection evidences this. He had a tangible physical body. People could touch Him. Jesus tells his disciples, "They were terrified and frightened, and supposed they had seen a spirit. And He said to them, "Why are you troubled? And why do doubts arise in your heart? Behold My hands, and My feet, that it is I Myself. Handle Me and see, for a spirit does not have flesh and bones as you see I have" (LK. 24:37-39). He ate food (Jn. 20:27). The apostle John emphasizes that Jesus' body surpassed physical limitations, as He appeared behind shut doors (Jn. 20:19). Jesus appeared on the road to Emmaus and then vanished (LK. 24:31). Scripture points out that our bodies will be like His. However, we must remember He is God, and we will not be a god (1 Cor. 15:42-44). We will have a resurrected body. Our bodies will be free from limitations and decay. The most important characteristic of our bodies is perfection and completeness. We will feast at the marriage supper of the Lamb (Rev. 19:9). Paul tells us that our spirit is willing, but our bodies and minds are weak (Rom. 7:14-25), but that will change with our new resurrected body. Our resurrected bodies will be what God intended them to be. All of this means we are complete in every way. We will have our five senses. They are a part of what makes us human. We will not only possess five senses, but we will also experience enhancements in them. Dr. Alcorn says regarding our senses, "I expect they will increase in their power and sensitivity."[2] I can imagine walking through a grassy field and really feeling it for the first time and hearing the birds sing like I had never heard before. The most beautiful sky that my mind cannot even behold. Our bodies and minds will be complete, and we can only imagine the joys that they will bring. The smells, the colors, the sounds, and the abilities. The Psalmist says, "I praise You, for I am fearfully and wonderfully made; Marvelous are Your works, And that my soul knows fully well" (149:14). We will experience wonders beyond our imagination, because of our enhanced senses. There is no question of identity. As it was from the beginning, God created male and female, and complete in all aspects of male and femaleness. Dr. Alcorn quotes from Joni Eareckson Tada, "I still can hardly believe it. With shriveled, bent fingers, atrophied muscles, gnarled knees, and no feeling from the shoulders down, I will one day have a new body, light, bright, and clothed in righteousness—powerful and dazzling. Can you imagine the hope this gives someone with a spinal cord injury like me? Or someone who has cerebral palsy, brain-injured, or who has multiple sclerosis? Imagine the hope this gives someone who is manic-depressive. No other religion or philosophy promises new bodies, hearts, and minds. Only in the Gospel of Christ do hurting people find such incredible hope."[3]

Will we remember our life on earth?

This question of memory has always been important to me and, most likely, to each of us. Without memories, we are no longer who we are. Ask any family that has had a loved one with dementia, and they will tell you that dementia robs them of their loved one's identity. Saying we do not have our memory is to remove who we are. Some try to say we only remember the good things, but that robs our history and identity. Some people wish they did not have some of their memories. When

Samuel appeared to King Saul, he knew who Saul was and what Saul had done. Samuel remembered. As Samuel knew what was happening in Saul's life, God could have briefed him, but Samuel remembered Saul. In Luke 9, Moses and Elijah speak about Jesus' departure. They were not less aware but more informed.

Some have suggested that those in heaven know what is happening on earth. Does using illustrations from the book of Revelation, which is filled with symbolism, prove people in heaven know what is happening on Earth? We can say that there is rejoicing in heaven when one sinner repents. (LK. 15:10). We can conclude that people and heaven know, but we cannot say for sure how they know. Perhaps God makes them aware when joyful events happen. Maybe He gives those believers with Him a window of joy, seeing loved ones at joyful times. Memory in God's presence takes on a whole new understanding.

As others point out, I believe we are not more ignorant in heaven but more knowledgeable. As worship in praise, prayer is essential in our lives. It is also vital in heaven. That being true, prayers of loved ones in heaven should encourage us, knowing we have prayers happening for us. How joyful that should make us feel knowing loved ones with Christ have not forgotten about us, and why would they not be concerned? Because they loved you on Earth, their love has now become enriched. The rich man was worried for his family. Why wouldn't saints in heaven be concerned about their loved ones? Paul says we have a great cloud of witnesses (Heb. 12:1). Going into the presence of Christ makes them care even more. Our loved ones are not with us physically, but we are with them more than we know. How often does a loved one in heaven ask about us? Those questions we cannot answer. Christ's care assures us they care. They cared on earth. Why would they care less in heaven? As scholars pointed out, praying is talking to God; we will not speak less to God in heaven but more. Knowing I have a father and grandparents talking to God about me is joyous. I must reiterate we do not pray to them. They have no power. They cannot answer any prayer. As scripture declares, "My help comes from the Lord, the maker of heaven and earth" (Ps. 121.1). Perhaps these are some unknown blessings when your family has a relationship with Christ. Paul writes, "For now we see in a mirror, dimly, but then face to face. Now I know in part, but then I shall know just as I also am known." (1 Cor. 13:12). When will that happen? Paul tells us when we are in Christ's presence. Let us remember we never pray to our loved ones for help. We miss them. We remember them. But our help cometh from the Lord.

Not only will we have new bodies that never get sick and never experience pain, but they will also have all those positive qualities of joy and laughter.

Will we have emotions? Someone may ask if we will have tears. Yes, tears of joy. The Bible says, "He will wipe away every tear from their eyes, and death shall be no more, neither shall there be mourning, nor crying, nor pain anymore " (Rev. 21:4, ESV). Our emotions are also a reflection of who we are. But right now, sin affects our emotions. To be like God, we will have emotions. The Bible expresses our Heavenly Father's feelings. We feel Jesus' emotions as He journeys with His followers toward the cross. One great thing about our emotions is we will never battle them. We will never have the feeling of being out of control. No more hurt feelings. No more misunderstanding. No conflicts. When Christ arose from the grave, He remained who He was—and we will be, too. Mary knew who she clung to. Amid all this goodness, Christ reshapes and molds our true identities into what He intended us to be.

Are there Marriages and Families in Heaven?

A young bride was so nervous she said to her pastor, "I'm afraid I might not make it through the ceremony. The pastor soothed her and said, "When you enter the church tomorrow, and the processional begins, you will walk down the same aisle you've walked down many times before." Concentrate on that same aisle you've walked many times before. Concentrate on that aisle. When you get halfway down the aisle, you'll see the altar, where you and your family have worshiped for many years. Concentrate on that altar. Then, when you see your groom, the one you love. Concentrate on him.

The next day, the bride walked down the aisle with her chin up and eyes bright. But those along the center were surprised to hear her muttering repeatedly, "Aisle, altar, him. Aisle, altar, him." Many eyebrows raised as people thought she said, "I'll alter him."[4]

The above story brings a smile to our faces. It does, however, hold a lot of truth. When Adam and Eve disobeyed and went their way. Sin entered the world, and we are bound in sin from that point forward. Blame and discourse took rise. We became selfish, and sin has colored every aspect of our relationships. Sin occurs in power struggles, hurt feelings, misunderstandings, and clashes. Sin affects our understanding of our world, ourselves, and others. With that in mind, remember what the religious leaders were trying to do to Jesus. "Then the Pharisees went and plotted how they might entangle Him in His talk" (Matt. 22:15). They failed. "The same day, the Sadducees, who say there is no resurrection, came to Him and asked Him, saying, "Teacher, Moses says that if a man dies, having no children, his brother shall marry his wife and raise up offspring for his brother." And Jesus' response has caused many people to frown. "For in the resurrection they neither marry nor are given in marriage, but are like angels of God in heaven"

(Matt. 22:23-30). I even had people say they disliked what Jesus said. I love my wife! I love my family! I want us to be a family! There is marriage and family in heaven. I will explain this by beginning with this quote: "The institution of marriage in the Bible reflects a long history of sociological and cultural development, as to some stages of which there can be no absolute certainty."[5] The concept of marriage, as described in the Bible, has developed over a long period. There were Matriarchal marriages, where the wife/mother would stay with her kin and be visited by her husband. They also described marriage where the wife had her tent (home). Leah and Rachel had her tent [home] Gen. 31:33. Then, there was a patriarchal marriage in which the woman became property. The husband and the father had authority over the wife and daughter(s). The Hebrew word Baal means "husband" or "Lord," reflecting the husband's role within the marital relationship (Gen.20:3). Think of our society's understanding of marriage, and that differs. What would marriage be in the future? Keeping the lineage of the family line was most important to the Sadducee's understanding of marriage. That is happening in Matthew 22. The Sadducees approach Jesus with the wife having seven husbands. How the Sadducees viewed marriage is not what God intended it to be. In Ephesians 5, the apostle Paul describes Jesus telling slaves, wives, and husbands about a whole new kind of relationship which they nor even our day does not understand. "A man leaves his father and mother and is joined to his wife, and the two are united into one. This is a great mystery, but it is an illustration of the way Christ and the Church are one" (Eph. 5:30-32 NLT). There is no perfect relationship. Jesus wanted them to understand that a good relationship is dying to oneself and lifting another. He uses the example of Christ and the Church.

Sadducees came to Jesus thinking they understood marriage. They believed they had one of those gotcha moments. We gotcha now, Jesus! Who does she belong to now, Jesus? Jesus is saying you do not understand the relationship of marriage. Jesus goes against the understanding of what they considered marriage. Marriage was not ownership or property. Relationships in heaven do not rely on social and legal structures. Marriage is not based on procreation in heaven. Relationships in heaven are like Christ and the Church. The disciples could not grasp marriage when they heard about divorce. They said it was better not to marry. (Matt. 19:10-12). If you love someone on earth, do you think you will love them less in heaven?

Jesus responds to the Sadducees, "For in the resurrection, they neither marry nor are given in marriage, but are like the angels" (Matt. 22:30). Jesus is saying that there is a whole new type of understanding of a relationship. In Rev. 19:9, we read, "Then he said to me, "Write: 'Blessed are those who are called to the marriage supper of the Lamb!' And he says to me, "These are the true sayings of God." Therefore, we must put aside our understanding of marriage and think of a new type of relationship, like Christ and His bride. Relationships in heaven will be far richer in heaven.

Heavenly Father,
we bow our heads before You.
We thank You for Your love. It's Your love that gave us Jesus.
It's because of Jesus that we have hope.
His name is the sweetest of all names, because in Him, we have life—life abundantly.
There is much that is a mystery to us.
We thank You for Your word, for in Your word we discover marvelous wonders.
Open our eyes that we may see what awaits us, and in doing so, bring glory to Your name.
In Jesus' name we pray. Amen.

---

[1] Buttrick, George, Arthur, Dictionary of the Bible Vol. 2, Abingdon Press, Nashville, 1962, P. 657.

[2] Alcorn, Randy, Heaven, Tyndale House Publishers, Inc., 2004, P.407

[3] Alcorn, Randy, P. 414.

[4] Larson, Craig Brain & Elshof, Phyllis Ten, P. 252.

[5] IDB vol 3, P. 278.

Chapter Five

A Home I Did Not Imagine

"See, I will create new heavens and a new earth.

The former things will not be remembered, nor
will They come to mind." (Isa. 65:17, NIV). "As
the new heavens and the new earth that I make will

endure before me, declares the Lord, So will your

name, and descendants endure." (Isa. 66:22, NIV).

"But in keeping with his promise we are looking

forward to a new heaven and a new earth, where

righteous dwells." (2 Peter 3:13, NIV). "Then I

saw a new heaven and a new earth, for the old

heaven and the old earth had disappeared. And

the sea was also gone. And I saw the holy city,

the new Jerusalem, coming down from God out

of heaven like a bride beautifully dressed for her

husband." (Rev. 21:1-2, NLT)

When I was a young lad living in Waterville,
Nova Scotia, there was an iconic sight: a train
station. I remember the first time my brother and I
stepped inside. I heard tap tap tap as we entered. The

man there, whose name I cannot remember, told me that the tapping I heard was a message he was receiving. It amazed me how he understood that tapping sound. Those sounds meant nothing to me, but to the trained ear, the sound had meaning. There was a story I read some time ago.

A young man walked into a noisy office. In the background, a telegraph clacked away. A sign on the receptionist's counter instructed job applicants to fill out a form and wait until they were summoned to enter the inner office. The young man completed the form and sat down with other applicants. After a few minutes, he got up and entered the door to the inner office. The other applicants thought the man got impatient and took it upon himself to enter the inner office. Within a few minutes, the young man emerged, escorted by the interviewer, who announced that they had filled the job and thanked the others for coming. The other applicants began grumbling. Then one says, "Wait a minute—I don't understand. He was the last one to come in, and we never even got a chance to be interviewed, and he got the job. How can that be? The employer said, "I'm sorry, but all the time you've been sitting here, the telegraph has been ticking out the message in Morse code: If you understand this message, come right in. The job is yours."

God uses many means to show His care. God speaks through His word, the Holy Spirit, and sometimes uses friends. The apostle Paul proclaims the world speaks of His glory. Sometimes, we do not see the signs that proclaim God cares. I can picture the applicants entering the office and seeing people sitting there. Someone may have pointed to the sign to fill out the application form. Another may have said we are waiting for an interview. We listen to all kinds of sounds, but we often listen to the wrong voices. The last man to enter the office, he heard the correct voice over all the others. There is so much we hear in our world, and often, we do not hear the voice of God amid the hustle. We hear about the cross and what Jesus has done, but do we not hear nor understand how much love He has for us? The above scriptures tell us something new will happen: new heavens and a new earth. What does any of that mean?

To glimpse what God will do, we must look at what He did. Genesis chapter one is an excellent place to begin.

In the beginning God created the heavens and the earth. The earth was without form, and void; and darkness was on the face of the deep. And the Spirit of God was hovering over the face of the waters. Then God said, "Let there be light; and there was the light, that it was good; and God divided the light from the darkness. God Called the light Day, and the darkness He called Night. So the evening and the morning were the First day. (1:1-5).

From the beginning, we see God and His Spirit are there. The New Testament tells us Jesus was there, "In the beginning was the word...." (John 1:1). The description of what God the Trinity is doing continued, "Let there be...." letting us know that at the end of each "Let there be," is the end of and beginning of another day until we come to the six-day and God does something different. He says, "Let us make man in Our image, according to Our likeness; let them have dominion over the fish of the sea, over the birds of the air, and over the cattle, over all the earth and every creeping thing that creeps on the earth" (Gen. 1:26). God has done something different on the 6th day. God made humans like Himself. Crafted them and shaped them to look after what He had created. He stands back as an artist, looks at his canvas, and examines his work. You can picture the architect or the painter looking at what they had created to see if anything was wrong. I have nephews who are in the construction industry. When the project is complete, someone must sign off on it. The only knowledge I have of this process is what I read. Those in charge must follow specific steps before considering the building project completed:

1. The inspector or a team, often including project managers, architects, and engineers, examines to ensure that work complies with relevant building codes.

2. Someone creates a list detailing any remaining tasks or deficiencies.
3. If there are deficiencies, it is necessary to complete all corrections.
4. They conduct the final inspection to confirm the completion of all the work.
5. Then, the certificate of completion happens.
6. They officially hand over the project to the owner.

God is all these people: the architect, engineer, project manager, and builder. He stands back, examines it, and says it is good, not only good, but VERY GOOD. Scripture tells us that God rests only after six days as if He is glad of a job well done. God created with thought. He put logic into what He was doing. It is as if He looked at it, and He was delighted.

The first thing we learn from the Genesis story is God is methodical. All God's actions are purposefully driven, which is reflected in the orderly and coherent nature of the biblical texts. God, being who He is, never has to second guess what He does. All scripture is there for a reason and has cause and effect to rule and order. That very thought is carried into the New Testament, where Paul tells Timothy, "All Scripture is given by inspiration by of God, and is profitable for doctrine, for reproof, for correction, for instruction in righteous, that the man of God may be complete, thoroughly equipped for every good work" (2 Tim.

3:16-17). God's kingdom is order-based. It is logical and carefully crafted for our benefit. This same order applies to our world; if you jump off a bridge, there is an effect. When God gave his ten commandants, they were for our good. If we examine them, we will understand the cause and effect. He wants us to see this about Himself. He could have snapped his fingers, spoken it, and thought about it, and it would have happened. All of this, he tells us, is for our benefit. That He carefully created with thought.

God created with thought, planning, caring, and for a reason. It was not an afterthought. It was not a hastily designed creation. God has logic and reason. We have logic and reason. We do not always utilize it for our good and the good of humanity, but it is present because we were created in His image. Everything in the Bible is for a reason. These are not random words that came out of the mouths of people of God, but people empowered by God. God wants us to see that He carries forward this careful thought from the beginning of the Genesis story to the very end of the Scripture. God put thought into what He did; in doing so, He told us He cared. God hands it to those created in His image, Adam and Eve, and hands over His creation with conditions and responsibilities. Adam and Eve listened to the lie— "Did God really say…?" That same lie is happening today. I only believe what Jesus says! Jesus said He came to fulfill scripture, not destroy it. How often do we pick that which makes us comfortable? You may ask, what does this have to do with heaven? I believe it has very much to do with heaven. That is the earth God wanted us to live, work, rest, and experience Him. That was to be our home. Our goal was to grow intellectually, develop, and become a family on the earth—a family of God. We know what happened.

Adam and Eve believed they knew better than God. They listened to the lie of the serpent. When Adam and Eve sinned, sin affected them and carried forward from that point onward. It also affected the earth. Decay and troubles from that point were a sign of the cry of humanity and earth. That did not change who God is. It changed humanity and our planet, but there is still order. There are still rules and order. There is still cause and effect. God did not throw us away, although He could have destroyed it all. Our very being longs to be reconnected to the God who created us. A song by Johnny Lee, "Looking for Love in All the Wrong Places," is an example of the lostness inside us from being disconnected from God. The very darkness inside of us drives us away from God. We do look in all the wrong places.

Sin happened and tainted everything. Genesis 6 tells us that humanity got so bad God said enough is enough. The Flood happened, and with the worldwide flood, the world changed once again. The seas have become a place of life but also a place of chaos and danger. God tells us this story for a reason. Humanity, left alone, will never be what God wanted. A place of hope, caring, and abundant life. God once again gives hope by saving Noah and his family. With the flood came a new world. Water covers seventy-one percent of the earth. In Genesis 8, God makes a covenant with Noah. We soon arrive at chapter 11, and in this chapter, we see humanity still thinks its ways will lead to life. In v. 4 of this chapter, it tells what is happening. The people fear being scattered over the whole earth. And they say, "Come, let us build ourselves a city and a tower whose top is in the heavens; lest we be scattered abroad over the face of the whole earth." They are going against the very command of God. Chapter 10 is more than genealogy. Humanity is still God's people, whether they realize it. They are to fill the earth and be a blessing. Listen to what Dr. Roop says, "the city and tower are not an end in themselves, but a means to "prevent scattering" the people. "The whole earth works to create unity through human effort that is opposed to the intent of God's blessings."[1] The whole point of this story is to show that humanity is in darkness. Jesus says, "No one can come to Me unless the Father who sent Me draws him; and I will raise him up at the last day" (John 6:44). The world will never discover what they lost on its own. The rest of the Old Testament reveals what happens when we are apart from God and illuminates what is needed. Christ Jesus is the one who is required, as the very promise of Genesis 3:15 tells us. He gives us a future and a hope. He is our way back to God. The verses at the beginning of this chapter, "A Home I Did Not Imagine," tell us what God will do at the end—A new heaven and new earth.

Sin destroyed our relationship with God and with every creature on earth. Sin destroyed the very home God created for us, and God promises to restore a new relationship and give us a new home. As Dr. Alcorn writes, "The New Earth will not be a non-Earth but a real Earth. The Earth spoken of in Scripture is the Earth we know - with dirt, water, rocks, trees, flowers, animals, people, and a variety of natural wonders. An Earth without these would not be Earth."[2] It is exciting to think that we are not going to an unfamiliar place but a place we will call Home.

I can recall many years ago, my brother and his wife, my sister and her husband, my wife and myself, and our parents went camping. We went to the campsite in Blomidon, Nova Scotia. What I remembered most about that time was being together as a family. We all lived in different places. We had busy lives, but experiencing nature together was a bonus. The earth was supposed to be a home, a family. But because of going our way and doing our own thing, we have divisions, hatred, and wars, and humanity thinks it still knows better. What is ironic is that the famous atheist Richard Dawkins calls himself a cultural Christian. He enjoys and loves what Christianity brought but does not accept where it came from. He wants the benefits but none of the responsibilities that God puts forth. Instead, he is a scoffer. That is what the apostle Peter writes to the church, telling us to be aware of such people.

The apostle Peter writes to a church living in what we would call today modern-day Turkey. Christians appear to be living amidst a pagan society. In the first chapter, Peter clarifies why he is writing to the Christian church." What Peter was saying was, "*YOU MUST LIVE YOUR FAITH.*" The pluralistic society that Peter writes was closing in on the church, and it is easy to believe what we hear. It is easy to become discouraged and be complacent. We can listen to something so much; even though it's wrong and a lie, we overlook it. We become desensitized. Sadly, sometimes, we even accept it. Hitler was telling everyone Jews were not people. The belief that the Jews were evil eventually gained acceptance. In Chapter 3, there were scoffers, saying Christ is not returning. How long have we heard that? Peter tells them what the prophets spoke about such people. Remember the flood. God does not look at time as we do. Peter tells them to hold on to their faith and why God's word is true. Peter reminds them of God's work at creation and the flood. God can change things anytime and bring about His will if He chooses. God's will will be done. He reminds them that God is patient, but they must remember that God has the power to destroy.

Then Peter tells them that is what God will do, and He will do it with fire. Remember Sodom and Gomorrah (2 Peter 2:6). What is fire — it Purifies. When He does that, there will be new heavens and earth. John tells the church in Philadelphia, "He who overcomes, I will make him a pillar in the temple of My God, and He shall go out no more. And I will write on him the name of My God and the name of the city of God, the New Jerusalem, which comes down out of heaven from My God, And I will write on him a new name" (Rev. 3:12). "The Biblical imagery is not one of replacement of earth by heaven, but one of a new heaven and new earth which are unified where Jesus will be in the midst."[3] Scripture shouts loud and clear sin destroys. Sin shaped, distorted, and make what was good bad. Paul Marshall writes so profoundly when he says, "sin it is not sin that makes us bear children, but is sin that makes childbearing painful. It is not sin that attracts men and women, but it is sin that fills our relationships with control and suspicion. It is not sin that makes music, but it is sin that fills our songs with vanity and lust. It is not sin that constructs cities and towers, but it is sin that makes those towers a symbol of pride and power. It is not sin that causes human beings to live and love, to make music and art, to work and create, to plant and harvest, to play and dance, but it is that undercuts and perverts them all." And he further says, "what we need is not to be rescued from the world, not to cease being humans, not to stop caring for the world, not to stop shaping human culture. What we need is the power to do these things according to the will of God. We as well as the rest of creation, need to be redeemed."[4] Now, that is an earth/heaven I am looking forward to. The apostle John writes,

Now I saw a new heaven and a new earth,
for the first heaven and the first earth had passed away.
Also, there was no more sea.
Then I, John, saw the holy city, New Jerusalem,
coming down out of heaven from God,
prepared as a bride adorned for her husband.
And I heard a loud voice from heaven saying,
"Behold, the tabernacle of God is with men,
and He will dwell with them,
and they shall be His people.
God Himself will be with them and be their God."
(Rev. 21:1-4)

The imagery of the New Jerusalem coming down from heaven in Revelation 21 strongly suggests heaven and earth's unification. This image symbolizes God will fully integrate His dwelling place (heaven) with the renewed earth, showing the union of God with His people. This unification includes not just the Jewish nation, as the apostle Paul tells us that God has also included the Gentiles in His covenant by grafting them. "But some of these branches from Abraham's tree—some of the people of Israel—have been broken off. And you

128

Gentiles, who were branches from a wild olive tree, have been grafted in. So now you also receive the blessing God has promised Abraham and his children, sharing in the rich nourishment from the root of God's special olive tree. Well, you may say, those branches were broken off to make room to make room for me. Yes, but remember–those branches were broken off because they didn't believe in Christ. So don't think highly of yourself, but fear what could happen. For if God did not spare the original branches, he won't spare you either" (Rom. 11:17-21, NLT). Paul further tells us that Christ has broken down the dividing wall between Jews and Gentiles, creating one new humanity out of the two. However, God has not broken His promises to Israel. The New Jerusalem coming down also tells us our new home will have cities and beautiful architecture.

I expect you to have questions about this new home Jesus is preparing for us. Let me attempt to answer some more questions I can think of while recognizing that our new home, which Jesus is preparing for us, remains a mystery. We can find reassurance because Christ will live with us. How do we know that? John hears "a loud voice from heaven saying, behold, the tabernacle of God is with men, and He will dwell with them, and they shall be His people. God Himself will be with them and be their God "(Rev. 21:3). This corresponds to what the prophet Ezekiel declares, "*THE LORD IS THERE.*"

"The word See might be best translated as "Now hear this!" or "Attention!" What is announced with such fanfare is the presence of God."[5]

1. Will there be TIME in heaven? I believe there will be time. God is beyond space and time. His creation is not. It's the same as heaven. Heaven is not God. The gospel of John tells us, "In the beginning was the Word, and the Word was with God, and the Word was God. He was in the beginning with God. All things were made through Him, and without Him nothing was made that was made." (1:1-3). Scripture clearly shows God is beyond His creation. Without time, there is no music. Revelation 5:8-9 and 14:2-3 describe music and singing in heaven. Music, by its nature, involves rhythm, sequences, and timing. Therefore, music suggests a form of temporal order exists on the new earth. Time may differ from what we understand time to be. Time to us expresses age, decay, and hustle, and none of that exists in the new heaven.

2. The verses in Revelation say there is no more sea in the new earth. We know rivers are flowing from the throne of God. (Rev. 22:1-2). Let me suggest that perhaps something else is going on when it mentions no more sea—the word sea has a variety of meanings, "by hyperbole, to a large vase or basin, the sea of brass, brazen sea."[6] I Kings 7:23 refers

to a large basin when we read, "And he made the Sea of cast bronze, ten cubits from one brim to the other; it was completely round...." The Sea also referred to chaos, fear, and death. We are familiar with Jonah, and the Sea became so fierce that he told them to toss him into the sea (Jonah 1). Jesus is in the boat fast asleep while the storm tosses the boat, and the disciples fear for their lives, and Jesus calms the wind and waters (Matt. 8:23-27; Mk. 4:35-41). The apostle Paul was being transported as a prisoner to Rome and said everyone must stay on the ship and God will spare their lives (Acts 27). Considering the abundance of imagery in the book of Revelation, we should not hastily conclude, based on one verse, that there will be no more sea. It seems more fitting to say there is no more fear, chaos, and death because we know there are bodies of water flowing from the Throne of God. After the flood, the earth changed. As mentioned, water covers 71% of the planet. The seas are now different from the original creation.

We can see the same imagery in Rev. 21:23-25, "The city had no need of the sun or the moon to shine in it, for the glory of God illuminated it. The Lamb is its light. And the nations of those who are saved shall walk in its light, and the kings of the earth bring their glory and honor into it. Its gates shall not be shut at all by day there shall be no night there." We know the apostle John records this picture of the contrast between light and darkness. "But he who hates his brother is in darkness and walks in darkness, and does not know where he is going, because the darkness has blinded his eyes" (1Jn. 2:11). Therefore, it is possible to interpret the passage in Revelation 21, both literally and symbolically. Many times in scripture, both meanings are true. We can be confident that the beauty we currently have on our planet will be equally and more beautiful in the future heavens and earth.

3. What are we going to do there? God tells Adam to work in God's first creation: "Then the Lord God took the man and put him in the garden of Eden to tend and keep it" (Gen. 2:15). The idea of us working in heaven may seem strange. Many people may cringe at the thought of working. The reason is that work became a curse after Adam and Eve's fall into sin (Gen. 3:17). God will renew work and make it meaningful on the new earth, as He intended. We are created in God's image, and God Himself engages in work. The apostle John tells us Jesus works (Jn. 5:17). Today, people try to get out of work, and some believe I deserve even what I did not earn. Paul writes to the church at Thessalonica and tells them to avoid idleness and to work (2

Thess. 3). Work today can be tiring, meaningless, and drudgery. That is not the work we will have in our new home. Most cannot wait to finish work. Working in our new home will not be tiring and drudgery but meaningful and will bring pleasure to our existence. What we do has meaning and will be meaningful. Paul Marshall talks about what work should be today. "Our work itself is a divine service to others. We get sick, we drive on roads, we read newspapers, we eat hamburgers: those who provide for us are God's servants, whether they know it or not. Let us take this awareness of service, and this deeper appreciation of work, into our congregations, into our lives, and into our hearts."[7] That attitude we should have today and in our work. In our future home with Christ, work will bring pleasure. Many people enjoy being greeted by their pets at the end of their work today. And that leads to an important question?

4. Will there be pets in heaven on earth/heaven? Let me answer that question this way. Animals cannot sin; therefore, they do not experience any torment upon death. There were animals in God's first creation, and He saved some animals from the flood. I can conclude animals are essential to God's creation. Jesus tells His followers not to worry about their basic needs. He uses the

example of the birds. "Look at the birds of the air, for they neither sow nor reap nor gather into barns; yet your heavenly Father feeds them. Are you not of more value than they" (Matt. 6:26). Animals are a part of our lives, reflect God's love, and contribute to the beauty and character of creation. The fall of Adam and Eve affected every part of creation, and God will make this new. God loves His children very much, so all things are possible with Him. The prophet Isaiah speaks of a glorious time when "The wolf also shall dwell with the lamb, The leopard shall lie down with the young goat, The calf and the young lion... And a little child shall lead them" (Isa. 11:6-7). Even though some suggest that this is happening during the millennial kingdom, there is no reason it would not continue in God's new creation. There is no good reason your beloved pet would not be in heaven.

5. Will we need to rest in God's new creation? After the 6th day, God rested. The Bible tells us that God rested for a reason. I previously stated everything we have in the Bible is for a reason. God rested to tell us something. Rest in Genesis carries several layers of meaning: completion of work, sanctification of time where God sets apart the 7th day as holy, and rest as a model for us to follow. Rest goes beyond physical rest. It goes beyond

attending church on a particular day, which is essential. Rest in the Biblical sense can also depict enjoying what one has and feeling gratitude for God's goodness. An understanding of thankfulness and recognizing all goodness comes from God. We have what we have because of His mercy and goodness. As someone has said, when I walk in nature, I am so thankful for the beauty and goodness of God. It shows reflection, acknowledgment, and gratitude. We grow that inner peace that God wants us to have as we rest (Ecc. 3:12-13; Ps. 92:1-4; Deut. 5:12:15; Ps. 23:1-3). Rest is essential as we thank God for His mercy and goodness; that same understanding will carry into our new resurrected lives. Rest for our physical bodies is necessary. Our Resurrected bodies will be incorruptible in the new creation, so resting takes on a deeper reflective meaning, enjoying God's mercy (1 Cor. 15:51-53). People always ask, "Will we sleep in heaven?" Some say no because we will have perfect bodies, but we know there will be a big banquet. Food is not to keep us alive. It is for joy and celebration; perhaps the same can be said about sleep. All we do will be for Joy in Christ. If we sleep, it is not because we have to but because we want to. It will be a gift from God.

6. What about babies? Are they in heaven? The answer is yes. In the Gospel of Matthew, Jesus discusses relationships and the importance of children. In the Bible, children are often portrayed as blessings from God (Ps. 127:3-5; Deut.6:6-7; Pr. 22:6). Ancient cultures sacrificed and discarded children to their gods. People in ancient cultures considered children valuable and pure, so they sacrificed them to gods. God forbade the practice of child-sacrificing. A common phrase in my younger days was, "Children should be seen and not heard." Jesus explicitly clarifies that children are essential to God's kingdom. "Then little children were brought to Him [Jesus] that He might put His hands on them and pray, but the disciples rebuked them. But Jesus said, "Let the little children come to Me, and do not forbid them; for such is the kingdom of heaven" (Matt. 19:13-14). Once again, we hear King David's words when his infant son died: "I shall go to him, but he shall not return to me" (2 Sam. 12:23). Children, until they reach the age of accountability, are under the cross. That age of accountability varies per individual. We will grow in knowledge as we fellowship together and under God's guidance. Are babies still babes in heaven, or are they fully mature? That question will have to remain a mystery. The most important question comes

with the idea of children: is their marriage in heaven? As seen in ancient times, there would be no more ownership regarding marriage. There will be no more childbirths. But relationships will always remain strong. That fact we can count on God is relational. Relationships are vital to God, not only now, but will continue in the New Heaven and New Earth. As these relationships unfold, we can find reassurance in their potential for excitement and continual growth. A perfect relationship in heaven is mind-blowing to me.

7. Will we pray in heaven? We may think prayer is unnecessary in heaven because we are there with God. We know there is worship in heaven. According to the book of Revelation, people worship and will worship God. We will worship God in all we do. Our very lives will be an act of worship. We know prayer is talking to God, so we can assume there will be prayer in heaven. I have grandparents and a father praying for me. Our loved ones talk to Jesus about us. Our loved ones inquire about us and hope to one day celebrate with us.

We must venture into two areas: who will be in this new heaven and earth? What is waiting for us at judgment?

Judgment Seat of Christ/ The Great White Throne Judgment

All the nations will be gathered before Him, and He will separate them one from another, as a Shepherd divides his sheep from the goats. And He will set the sheep on His right hand, but the goats on the left. (Matt. 25:32-33).

In March 2007, in the Kuban region of southern Russia, at least sixty-two people were killed by a fire that quickly blazed through a home for the elderly. The greatest tragedy was that someone could have prevented the deaths.

Authorities say a night watchman ignored two fire alarms. When the third alarm sounded and the watchman saw flames, he finally took action to evacuate residents. Even then, other staffers were notably absent from their posts, making the escape effort nearly impossible. By the time fire authorities and rescue workers arrived, many residents had already died from smoke inhalation.[8]

When I was a young man working in the costing department of a local company, I became friends with another young man. We both believed we were Christians. I, from a more conservative background, felt there were certain activities I could no longer take part in. He thought he could do them and repent

138

afterward if they were wrong. I would ask my friend if you do those actions believing you can find forgiveness. Is that genuine repentance? I am following the proper procedure, was my friend's reply.

You are most likely puzzled by these two stories, wondering what they have to do with the title. In our first story, the watchman overlooked the signs, and people died. In the second story, we can assume my friend and I were hearing a message about how a Christian should live, but each heard a different message.

At least two critical messages run through both stories: actions and responsibilities. The second message is listening and hearing. We find those two stories relevant today because we constantly receive messages. The mainstream media no longer tells us what is happening. They have an agenda. They make the story fit their message. It is up to us to cipher what we hear. We can only do that through God's word. Paul tells Timothy, "Be diligent to present yourself approved to God, a worker who does not need to be ashamed, rightly dividing the word of truth" (2 Tim. 2:15). Both stories have another commonality: depending upon our actions and responsibility will determine our consequences.

In the text of Matthew 25, Jesus told his followers a parable about watching and being prepared for His return. Then, He talks about talents and what a person does with those talents will determine their accountability. Then we get to our text. Jesus is dividing two groups of people. He calls these two groups sheep and goats. The imagery would have been familiar to the listeners. Sheep are more docile and obedient, while goats are more independent and curious. Sheep were often seen as more valuable because of their wool than goats. The Bible frequently uses sheep to represent God's people. Jesus says, "My sheep hear My voice." One group is on the right, and the other is on the left. This right and left had significance. The right side was often associated with honor, power, favor, and blessings, while the left could relate to dishonor, disfavor, and rejection (Ps. 110:1; Matt. 26:64). Now, let us look at these two judgments:

Judgment Seat (BEMA) of Christ.

But why do you judge your brother? Or why do you show contempt for your brother? For we shall all stand before the judgment seat of of Christ. For it is written: "As I live, says the Lord Every knee shall bow to Me, And every tongue shall confess to God." So then each of us shall give account of himself to God" (Rom.14:10-12).

For we must all appear before the judgment seat
of Christ, that each one may receive the things
done in the body, according to what he has done,
whether good or bad" (2 Cor. 5:10).

The word Bema, spelled "βῆμα" in Greek, means "step" or "platform." In ancient Greece, the bema was a raised platform used by officials for public speaking, pronouncements, or judgments. An illustration of that is when the apostle Paul is in Athens, and he stands on Mars hill and tells them about "THE UNKNOWN GOD" (Acts 17:16-34). In ancient Greece, victors of athletic games or military conquest received crowns or other awards for their achievements. The word Bema became used for a tribune in the law courts of Greece.[9] All believers are to stand before and face judgment (Rom.). 14:10-12; 2 Cor. 5:10). It seems only fitting that the One who redeemed us examines our work. The heavenly Father has handed over all judgment to the Son. (Jn. 5:22-23).

If you find yourself here, Christ took your place upon the cross. You have received salvation as a gift, not as anything you have done. (Eph. 2:8-9). You are a part of the redeemed. Why are you here? The apostle John records the words of our righteous judge, "And behold, I am coming quickly, and My reward is with Me, to give to every one according to his work" (Rev. 22:12). The apostle Matthew records Jesus' words when the Pharisees and Sadducees were testing Him, always looking for signs. Their questioning was not to find the truth but to see if they could trick Him, and Jesus told His disciples to take heed of such people. He reminds the disciples about the feeding of the 5000. Jesus asks them who they say I am, and the apostle Peter says, "You are the Christ, the Son of the living God" (Matt. 16:16). Jesus tells Peter his awareness was not his doing, but the heavenly Father who revealed it to him. Once again, this reminds us that no one comes to Jesus unless the Father draws them (Jn. 6:44). He reminds the disciples that being His follower is a cost (Matt. 16:24). Jesus tells His followers that giving up and suffering for Him is nothing in compared of what He has in store for them, "For the Son of Man will come in the glory of His Father with His angels, and then He will reward each according to his works" (Matt. 16:27).

At the judgment seat of Christ, the redeemed recount what they did with their life. This procedure of providing an account takes place collectively and individually. That means, as far as you are concerned, it's you and the judge. Jesus often used parables to illustrate spiritual truths, including themes of obtaining and losing reward. The parable of the talents is but one example (Matt. 25:14-31). The parable illustrates the importance of being ready for Christ's return. We place this parable in what we call the Olivet Discourse. Jesus was on the

Mount of Olives. Today, the Mount of Olives is a prominent historical, religious, and geographical ridge. Its location is east of Jerusalem's Old City in modern-day Israel. Jesus had predicted the destruction of the Temple, which surprised and confused the disciples, leading them to ask about the signs of the end and His return. This scene is more profound than just looking for Christ's return. Jesus tells a parable to get its readers to ask what they have been doing with their lives. There are three servants: "And to one he gave five talents, to another two, and to another one, to each according to his own ability; and immediately he went away on a journey" (Matt. 25:15). We notice the master gave different amounts to each of the three servants. To prevent anyone from claiming unfairness, the master provided a reason for giving various talents according to the person's ability. It is not always wise to wish for more than you can handle. As the saying goes, when much is given, much is required. As followers of Christ, we have what we have, and we are where we are. We should not use that as an excuse for not growing in our faith and ability. God can use us where we are.

My mom and I talked some years back, and she wondered what her gift was. I am sure most of us have asked ourselves what our talent is. She used to send cards to people missing from church. Not only did she send cards, but she also wrote a personal note for each one. She showed the same devotion and care when she sent birthday cards to her children and grandchildren. The person doing it may view the task as insignificant, but to Jesus, you did it unto Him. My wife found Mom's personal touch a gift.

The crux of the parable is the willingness to risk for Christ. The parable's conclusion makes that clear. We discover one servant who refuses to acknowledge the gift and does nothing. Why does he do nothing? Out of fear. Doing nothing is not an option. Because of doing nothing, he loses. Then, we come to the dividing point—the separation on the left and right—between the sheep and the goats.

Moreover, those who used the gifts for humanity's benefit received commendation. They started as servants and ended as rulers. Now, it is our turn to be judged by the One who died for us. We do not have to give an account of our life before accepting Christ as Lord. The One who died for us has cleansed us of those sins.

I remember my brother and I first went fishing as young boys. We were heading to the north mountain where my dad grew up, which was approximately 20 kilometers away from where we lived in Waterville. We arrived, exited the vehicle, and Dad cut an alter for my brother, me, and himself. We wrapped some fishing twine and hook on the pole, lifted some rocks, found worms, and off we went on this adventure. Following the stream, getting wet was all a part of our journey. To top the day, we caught trout. I'm not sure who caught the most trout; most likely, it was Dad. That did not matter. The trout was the reward at the end of the adventure. In our lives, we may encounter both mishaps and blessings. It is not about the mishaps or the blessings but how we traveled the stream. It's not about the rewards. It's about the life we live.

At the judgment seat of Christ, we will give Christ an account of the road we traveled. The two primary verses under the above heading speak directly to our appearance before Christ's judgment. It is here we receive or lose our reward(s). The Judge Himself has already secured salvation.

We often misunderstand rewards for how many people we have led to Christ. Using a scale of 1 to 10, we would see Billy Graham as getting 10, for he preached worldwide and led the 1000s to Christ, and ourselves reaching the scale of 1. In 1992, Diane Sawyer interviewed Billy Graham. She asked him what he hoped people would say about him after he was gone. He says, "I don't want them to say big things about me because I do not deserve them. He said I want to hear one person say one thing about me, and that is the Lord. When I face Him, I want Him to say to me, "well done thy good and faithful servant, but I don't think I will." That may shock most of us. At this judgment, everything becomes clear. There are no secrets from the *JUDGE*. Luke chapter 8 reveals that God uncovers all secrets. Jesus tells the parable of the sower. The

Parable illustrates people's varied responses to the word of God. It highlights the importance of a receptive heart. One hears and quickly says no, that makes little sense to me, or that's not for me, is the response. Another hears and gets excited, believing for a while but not grounded in God's word. Life trials may arise, not rooted in God's word, and they become discouraged. With the lack of spiritual growth and life worries, they turn away. The third group fed their heart with prayer, worship, and God's word, and when trials and difficulties came, they persevered and produced growth. Jesus says all the whys, ifs, and buts will be revealed— Nothing will be hidden (v. 17).

During the first missionary efforts to China, Matteo Ricci, a 16th-century Italian Jesuit priest, saw a few converts. James Hudson Taylor, a notable missionary to China in 1865, substantially impacted China. The apostle Paul writes to the Corinthians, "One plants, another waters" (1 Cor 3:6-9). The Church had divisions regarding who was the most influential in doing God's work. Paul tells them they are viewing things incorrectly. He is saying each has a role to play. The key factor in Paul's statement is God. It is God who does the growth. It is God who quickens the heart. God provides, and we do; the fruit is up to Him.

We can look at the entire process of rewards in the same way as salvation. Jesus says, "No one can come to Me unless the Father who sent Me draws him, and I will raise him up at the last day" (Jn. 6:44). No one can take credit for our salvation, for it is a gift from God, and in the same way, whatever we do planting or watering it is God doing the harvesting. All this means that every effort that is made, no matter how big or small, in our eyes, is God's work. Because of that, God chose to give blessings (rewards) collectively and individually. If we are at this judgment, we are giving an account of our life as followers of Christ.

In Matthew 25:37-40, the final judgment in Matthew's gospel, Jesus, says, when you fed the poor, helped those in need, etc. All of that is doing my work. You could say that many charitable organizations are doing good things. That is true. If they recognize it or not, all goodness comes from God. Any kind deed is an act from God. God has used even the ungodly to pour forth His mercy. I would suggest that to understand Matthew 25 fully, we must recognize who Jesus is talking to—His followers. He comes out of the temple and, in Matthew 24, tells His disciples what will happen in the future. Therefore, Christians are to do this kindness, and doing so reflects Christ. God judges us based on our opportunities, and we leave the fruit to Him. Those who are overcomers receive the rewards.

Matthew and Mark's gospel tells us that James and John wanted to be rewarded with the honor of sitting on Jesus' right and left. I can easily picture the mom coming to Jesus and making this request. We all want the best for our children, but again, we do not understand the nature of these rewards: to be great, be a servant, and first become a slave (last). There is a cost involved. Jesus tells them you know not what you are asking. We consider the benefits but do not want the costs. What I will do is worth what I will give up; that is how we usually make our decisions. Jesus evaluates what we did in the light of the Gospel, thus reward.

Rewards are gifts of God's grace. God convicts the heart, → the person responds. The more the person responds (service), → closer we get to Christ. The closer we get to Christ, → the more He uses us. From all of that comes rewards for our service. He did not need to give rewards. Life eternal is the greatest gift of all. Rewards result from our service and an expression of God's love.

The first question you may ask is, I have only been a Christian for a short time, and if Christ returns, my reward will be little. Once again, we see the rewards incorrectly. Rewards are not setting up classes of haves and have-nots. Everyone rejoices with each other. Matthew 20, Jesus tells a parable of workers starting at different times but all receiving the prize. Like the thief on the cross, some individuals will experience salvation at the last moment. Others will return to Christ through fire and lose their reward. Most of us in the Western world have had many opportunities to serve. God gives us opportunities, and we can bury them or use the opportunity to serve. We can do little or much. God knows all and will reward accordingly. The apostle Paul speaks to a divided Church, "If anyone's work which he has built on it endures, he will receive a reward. If anyone's work is burned, he will suffer loss; but he himself will be saved, yet so as through fire" (1 Cor. 3:14-15). Fire symbolizes the judgment and testing of one's work. Scripture clarifies that the all-knowing God sees every motive, selfish act, and hidden thing.

I am sure you want to know the reward(s) for serving Christ. Rewards give us privileges. You can receive various crowns for serving Christ: the Crown of Righteousness, the Crown of Glory, the Crown of Life, and the Crown of Rejoicing. What is a Crown? In ancient Greek culture, they awarded wreaths or crowns to victors in athletic competitions as a symbol of honor and gave them privileges. In a new heaven and earth context, Crowns offer ruling privileges. We may have a role of governing in the eternal kingdom of God. Revelation 20:4-6 mentions that believers will co-ruler with Christ. This concept of co-rulership suggests that believers will have roles of authority and responsibility in the administration of God's eternal kingdom. Some see this as ruling in the Millennial kingdom. Christ promised twelve thrones to the twelve apostles, but there may also be other thrones that people will occupy. If not, God will give us various responsibilities and assignments that correspond to our faithfulness while living on this planet.[10] Dr. Alcorn makes life in God's new creation exciting when He says, "I believe the New Earth will offer us opportunities we wished for but never had. God's original plan was for humans to live happy and fulfilling lives on Earth. If our current lives are only chances at that, God's plan has been thwarted. Consider the injustices—many honest, faithful people never got to live fulfilling lives, while some dishonest and unfaithful people seemed to fare much better. But God is not unjust, and this is not our only chance at life on Earth. The doctrine of the New Earth clearly demonstrates that."[11] God takes everything into account. The sermon on the mount demonstrates the hope of fulfillment. To appreciate what is waiting at the judgment seat of Christ, we must try to get a glimpse of what may happen at The Bema seat. I believe the illustration I will present is a must. It is an individual occurrence. Some individuals may be less dramatic depending upon your closeness to the Savior. No matter how close, none of us followers of Christ are perfect, as Billy Graham saw himself fall short, for we do not fully grasp what Christ has done for us. This scene is through my eyes. In this scene, the sacrificial lamb has taken His rightful place on the throne, and it is Him we must come before. He was the promised one of Genesis 3:15. He is the beginning and the ending, as John calls the Alfa and Omega.

I would like you to return to Christ's judgment seat with me. I want you to picture what I see and what I feel. Perhaps even look through my eyes, see yourself, and experience how you may feel. I have arrived, and excitement and chatter fill the air as we all wait for the king of kings. The trumpet sounds. The rest of the angels stand at attention as Christ enters and sits on the throne. No one needs to tell me what I must do. With shaking knees, I bow in awe. Even bowing seems insufficient. I drop face down on the floor; I try to hide my face. I attempt to hide myself by curling into a fetal position, but those piercing eyes observe everything, leaving nothing concealed. Although I hide from the throne, the glory blinds me. There is nowhere to hide.

I have never seen or experienced anything like this. My mind is overflowing trying to grasp the Righteousness, Majesty, and glory. I thought I understood what Christ did for me on the Cross, but I did not. I know how unworthy I am. All my failures flashed before my face. It was so engulfing that I thought it would swallow me. My weeping is so overwhelming that I cannot stop. I see all the missed opportunities, misspoken words spewing from my mouth, and all the times I justified my actions were racing before my mind, all the times I allowed my fear to stop me from doing what I knew Christ wanted me to do and it felt like my heart would explode. He knew *EVERYTHING*. I could not get my breath! Tears would not stop. My heart hurt. If I could die 1000 deaths, I would still experience nothing like I do now. Why did I, at times, listen to the wrong voices? Why did I allow myself to think those things would bring me peace? Why was I so selfish? W*hy—Why—Why*! Jesus, *HELP ME* were words that finally sprung from deep inside me. Those same words that gave me a new life when I asked Christ to be my Lord and forgive my sins were before me. At that moment, I fully knew what Christ did for this sinner. At that very moment of judgment, I understood Christ's *LOVE*. I knew He was the perfect judge, and His judgment was just and true. I experienced my tears being wiped away. I had no more pain. As my former life passed away, I felt embraced in the arms of my Savior. I experienced love like I had never experienced before. The feeling of safety washed over me as I found refuge in Christ's arms. I thought I knew what saved meant. I experienced a sense of wholeness as I comprehended the Bible terms: saved, being saved, and will be saved. All of us, redeemed, tossed our crowns before Him because He had given it all. Those rewards were because of Him, and to Him, they belong.

All those talents were gifts that came from Him. We knew that any good we did was Him doing it through us. He was so merciful and loving. He rewarded us. It is amazing! I am a mere sinner, deserving of nothing and yet receiving everything. "And God will wipe away every tear from their eyes; there shall be no more death, nor sorrow, nor crying. There shall be no more pain, for the former things have passed away" (Rev. 21:4). We rejoice collectively in fellowshipping because of the rewards our brothers and sisters receive. There are no thoughts of rewards or greatness. We understood and looked forward to growing more in Christ.

Father open our eyes, soften our hearts, quicken

Our ears that we may be sensitive to what happens

At the The Great White Throne Judgment. In doing so

We may work and pray harder. In Christ's Name, we Ask.

The Great White Throne Judgment

Then I saw a great white throne and Him
who sat on it, from whose face the earth
and the heaven fled away. And there was
found no place for them. And I saw the
dead, small and great, standing before God,
and books were opened. And another book
was opened, which is the Book of Life. And
the dead were judged according to their works,
by the things which were written in the books.

The sea gave up the dead who were in it, and
Death and Hades delievered up the dead who
Were in them. And they were judged, each one
According to his works. Then Death and Hades
Were cast into the lake of fire. This is the second
Death. And anyone not found written in the book
of Life was cast into the lake of fire. (Rev. 20:11-
15).

Before discussing the Great White Throne judgment, I must point out that I have lumped all the judgments into two. Some scholars see judgment happening in an eschatological timeline. The rapture of the church → Judgment Seat of Christ → Great Tribulation → Judgment of the nations → Millennial Kingdom → Great White Throne Judgment. I have tried not to disgust timelines. Why, you may ask? The outcome of the Sheep and Goats Judgment and the Great White Throne Judgment are the same in determining eternal destiny. "The separative aspects of the last judgment point to the separate destinies of the saved and the lost, the righteous and the unrighteous, the redeemed and the unredeemed."[12] They have rejected Christ, and every aspect of their life is being examined and judged. The primary emphasis on distinguishing these two judgments does not revolve around reconciling the eschatological timeline. Matthew 25 is in the context of parables emphasizing preparedness, for we do not know the hour of Christ's return. And what we do with our life matters. Jesus is pointing out that judgment is waiting for all. Therefore, timelines are unnecessary in understanding judgment and its Consequences. We cannot understand what happens to unbelievers without discussing the Great White Throne Judgment.

This day of judgment permeates the entire Bible. The Bible often calls this final judgment "The day of judgment" (Am. 5:18-20; Zeph. 1:14; 1 Thess. 5:2; 2 Peter 2:9; 3:7). The Bible also refers to it as "the day of Christ" or "the day of the Lord" (I Cor. 18; 2 Cor. 1:14; Phil. 1:6, 10). Jude calls it "the great day" (Jude 6). John the Baptist comes on the scene shouting repentance for the wrath that is to come. This judgment that is to come is universal. Not only does it affect the entire world, but death seals it. We saw earlier that God created everything perfect, and Adam and Eve sinned, and that sin entered the world and resulted in judgment. The judgment day has come, and it serves as a reminder that those who chose their path, not Christ, and those who chose evil cannot escape. God will judge every deed and will right all wrongs. Satan's attempt to dethrone God has failed, and now all those who replaced God with something else are being held accountable. Again, we must point out that this judgment is unlike man's. It is not uncommon to turn on the news and hear a person questioning the fairness of the judgment. It is not unusual to hear people questioning the fairness of the judgment based on whether the judge is a Republican, Democrat, Liberal, or conservative. There will be no questioning of the authority of the fairness of this judgment.

We come to this event with a saddened heart. How can we not experience a heart filled with sorrow? This judgment is not one of rejoicing. It is not a temporary sadness. It does not bring joy but separation. This judgment is like the Judgment Seat of Christ. That similarity ends with Christ being the judge. It is fitting because the rejected One sits on the throne and is about to pass a sentence. Despite Christ's innocence, they sentenced Him to a demoralizing death. He willingly went to the cross and, in doing so, demonstrated God's love. He went there to take our place and offer life. All scripture points to this day.

I am discussing this event and cannot help but feel a broken heart. To think of one person being here is painful, and it is even more painful when you consider those you love may end here.

When writer Mitch Albom heard that his favorite college professor, whom he hadn't seen in twenty years, was dying of Lou Gehrig's disease, he began visiting him weekly. In his bestselling book Tuesdays with Morrie, Albom describes their visits, focusing on his old professor's wit and insights. One time, Mitch asked Morrie why he bothered following the news since he wouldn't be around to see how things turned out. Morrie responded, "It's hard to explain, Mitch. Now that I'm suffering, I feel closer to people who suffer than I ever did before. The other night on TV, I saw people in Bosnia running across the street, getting fired on. I just cried. I feel their anguish as if it were my own. I don't know any of these people. But—how can I put this? I'm almost drawn to them."[13]

I think we all can identify with Morrie. When we walk a hard road, it is, then we seem to understand. Whenever I had the privilege of sitting by the side of a dying person without taking away their feelings, I could almost feel what they must have been feeling. If they allow you to get that close, in some small way, you identify with them. And you hurt with them. It reminds me of the apostle Paul's words, declaring he looked forward to going with the Lord. But that faith did not take away his grief for his companion. "I consider it necessary to send to you Epaphroditus, my brother, fellow worker, but your messenger and the one who ministered to my need; For indeed he was sick almost unto death; but God had mercy on him, and not only on him but on me also, lest I should have sorrow upon sorrow" (Phil. 2:25-27). Paul saw that Epaphroditus healing was a gift to him. Relationship matters. Sadness hurts. Therefore, thinking about the Great White Throne Judgment is challenging, especially when feeling a heart cry. Heart's cry, we do feel.

I can assume Christ takes His seat as a judge with a heavy heart. These are the people He bled for. He felt every lash so they could have life, and He must pass sentence on them. It is also fitting-Vengeance is mine, declares the Lord (Rom. 12:19-21). The writer to the Hebrews highlights the seriousness and gravity of facing God's judgment, particularly when a person has rejected His grace and mercy. "For we know Him who said, "Vengeance is Mine, I will repay," says the Lord. And again, "The Lord will judge His people." It is a fearful thing to fall into the hands of the Living God" (Heb. 10:30-31).

There is no contradiction between God's heartfelt sorrow and His justice. Paul writes to the Roman Church, "For God presented Jesus as the sacrifice for sin. People are made right with God when they believe that Jesus sacrificed his life, shedding his blood. This sacrifice shows that God was being fair when he held back and did not punish those who sinned in times past, for he was looking ahead and including them in what he would do in this present time. God did this to demonstrate his righteousness, for he himself is fair and just, and he makes sinners right in his sight when they believe in Jesus" (Rom. 3:25-26, NLT). I once saw this role of Christ being a judge over those who judged Him as a fitting payback. That is true and much more.

How wrong I was. Yes, it is fitting, but Christ approaches this task with a broken heart. Why do I now view the judgment differently? Is it because I am not better than the unbelievers? The difference is that I received the gift Christ offered, and they rejected Christ. Humans do not always separate anger and compassion, mercy and justice very well. God has no difficulty. Christ comes with a heavy heart and a hand of righteous justice. God's character magnifies His holiness, love, and justice and cannot be separated, for He is who He is—*"I AM WHO I AM"* (Ex. 3:14). Jesus echoed those very words about Himself when he was told the religious leaders who He was, "Most assuredly, I say to you, before Abraham was, I AM" (Jn. 8:58).

We are moral beings. We are sensitive to right and wrong, good and bad, justice and injustice. Why? God made us in His image. When Adam and Eve fell into disobedience, their disobedience infected that image and spread it worldwide. As Dr. John Lennox, Oxford Mathematician and scientist, says, we are more than DNA. If we are only a product of our DNA, there is no right or wrong, no good or evil. In one of Dr. Lennox's lectures, he says God takes a risk in creating us in His image. He didn't want robots. He wanted a relationship with people who could say yes or no. Whether we realize it, that is what we do. Loving someone comes with the risk of having that love rejected. God took a risk in loving us. We know some people do not accept rejection very well. We read about, heard of, or known of individuals who have tried to coerce someone into loving them. They stock, threatened, and sometimes even killed the person and themselves. That is not loving. God offers His love, not force it. He gives people what they desire: separation from Him if that is what they choose. He judges and gives them what they want.

At twenty-eight, Tom Brady has won three Super Bowls and was ranked as

One of the best quarterbacks ever. But it isn't enough. "Why do I have three Super Bowl rings and still think there's something greater out there for me?" He asks in a 2005 interview. "I mean, maybe a lot of people would say, "Hey man, this is what it is. I reached my goal, my dream, and my life. I think, God, it's got to be more than this. I mean, this isn't, this can't be, what it's all cracked up to be."[14]

We have all been there. Thinking of the new job, new house, the great vacation, and pay raise will all make life worthwhile. It did not matter if I was a teenager, thinking about my first car, my place, and the perfect girlfriend. Then I would be living. That thinking does not end with being a teenager. I wish we all would grow out of thinking that all we need to do is fill our life with something. We do that because we are empty. That emptiness does not pass just because we want it to or when we fill it with something. We are unaware that we are lost. A philosopher asks, "Does a fish know it is in water?"

Some say it was Aristotle who asked that question. I do not think so, and it does not matter who asked, but it describes our lostness. The answer is, "Not until it is out of water." That same illustration can apply to us.

We are sinful people born in a fallen world and do not know what is wrong with us. We are a part of a fallen world that is opposed to God. Just as a fish notices being in water only when it is removed, we realize being part of a fallen world, opposed to God, only when we are separate from it. That is what the apostle Paul's message to the Ephesian Church declares. Paul says, you once were dead but are now alive. You once had a film over your eyes, but now you see. You did not know that you were living according to the world. Your very nature opposed God. You were on the path to destruction, but because of God's mercy, you are no longer those people. What is so merciful about Christ? He did that out of His love. It was not our doing it. That is when we can appreciate the fish illustration, "For by grace you have been saved through faith, and that not of yourselves; it is the gift of God" (2 Eph. 2:1-9).

The writer of Ecclesiastes says he tried it all and cries, "Vanity of Vanities, all is vanity whether good or evil." He concludes, "For God will bring every work into judgment, Including every secret thing, Whether good or evil" (12:14). No matter how much more we desire, it never fills that void where something is absent. We never question why; if we do, it is only momentary, and then we try to fill that hole with something.

My sister gave me a journal titled "Dream Big," which lies on a rack by my recliner. When I read, hear an interview, or have a thought worth considering, I write it down in my Dream Big journal. I will write what the speaker said, the context in which it was spoken, and my thoughts on the matter. Dr. Lennox was talking about the existence of God and the value of humans. Even die-hard atheists believe in the value of human worth. Our inner drive for justice and our passion for love represent something greater than ourselves. Dr. Lennox said One of the most important things is the concept of justice. The Christian says there will not be any old justice but a righteous judgment. We have arrived at The Great White Throne Judgment (Rev. 20:11). I can hear someone say my sin is not that big. I will illustrate what I listened to my pastor say. If I tell a lie to my children, there will be little consequences except perhaps disappointment. If I tell a lie to my wife, I will experience consequences. If I tell a lie to a police officer, I may find myself before a judge. If I tell a lie before a judge, it matters more. We see our sins as minor. God, who is holy, who the angels cry holy, holy, abhors sin, and there are consequences. His Son would not have gone to the Cross if sin was not grave.

This judgment takes place before the creation of the New Heavens and the New Earth. The present earth and heaven have ceased. The apostle Peter told us that would happen. "But the heaven and the earth which are now preserved by the same word, are reserved for fire until the day of judgment and perdition of ungodly" (2 Peter 3:7). Peter is dealing with skeptics and mockery of Christ's return. He continues his argument, saying God destroyed the world with flood. This time, He is going to do it with fire. He says God is patient, but His patience will end, and it will come when you least expect it. Everything passing away will create a tremendous noise, and all the scoffers will face judgment (10-12). In our text, that day has arrived, and the first casualty is Satan.

This chapter began with Satan being bound, loosened for a time, and finally tossed into the lake of fire. "The devil, who deceived them, was cast into the lake of fire and brimstone where the beast and the false prophet are. And they will be tormented day and night forever and ever" (Rev. 2010). The final judgment had happened to him. Satan does not need to come before the judgment throne of God. Why? Isaiah the prophet describes a scene of the fall of Lucifer and his judgment. Satan is but one of several names that he has. Other names traditionally associated with Satan, Devil (Matt. 4:1; 1 Peter 5:8). Beelzebub (Matt. 12:24), Prince of the Power of the Air (Eph. 2:20), Dragon (Rev. 12:9), Accuser of the brethren (Rev. 12:10), Father of lies (Jn. 8:44), Prince of this world (Jn 12:31), Adversary (1 Peter 5:8). Prophet Isaiah tells of his judgment,

"How you are fallen from heaven, O Lucifer,

a son of the morning! How you are cut down

to the ground, You who weakened the nations!

For you have said in your heart: I will ascend

into heaven, I will exalt my throne above the

stars of God; I will also sit on the mount of the

congregation On the farthest side of the north;

I will ascend above the heights of the clouds,

I will be like the Most High. Yet you shall be

Down to sheol, To the lowest depths of the

Pit." (Isa. 14:12-15).

People often interpret the prophet Ezekiel 28:12-17 as references to the fall of Satan, describing his pride, rebellion against God, and subsequent judgment. John mentions Jesus talking about the judgment that has already passed on Satan. "Now is the judgment of this world; now the ruler of this world will be cast out" (Jn. 12:31). In chapter 16 of John's Gospel, Jesus talks about His departure and the coming of the Holy Spirit. He mentions that when the Holy Spirit comes, He will convict the world, and Jesus declares He has already passed judgment on Satan. "Judgment will come because the ruler of this world is already judgment" (11, NLT). In the book of Revelation, John describes a battle in heaven where Satan is expelled (12:7-9). The first book tells us of the promised "ONE" coming who would battle this serpent, and the conclusion has happened. God throws Satan into the lake of fire. "The devil, who deceived them, was cast into the lake of fire and brimstone where the beast and the false prophet are. And they will be tormented day and night forever and ever" (Rev. 20:10). Revelation depicts the lake of fire as a place of final judgment and eternal punishment for Satan, the beast, and the false prophet. This place of everlasting punishment is the ultimate destination for all evil. It is called the second death—the powerful symbolism gulfs us with the idea of a body of water, purifying and destroying. Perhaps the point is to make us remember the flood and the destruction of Sodom and Gomorrah. This scene possibly contrasts that with the added imagery. In 79 AD, Pompeii, in modern-day Sicily, the eruption of Mount Vesuvius near the Roman cities of Pompeii and Herculaneum was the most famous, turning Pompeii into utter ash.

In June 2018, my wife, four other family members, and I went to Italy. We stayed in Termina, Sicily, which was full of life. It seems strange that 55 km away, everything had the imprint of death— of Mt Etna. It was fascinating to walk upon the hard, dry, brittle ash. The scene looked lifeless where we walked, and outside the hardened lava were signs of life. That is the picture the apostle John wants us to see: a place not of dry, hardened lava but a picture that is engulfing, living, and burning. A fire that never ends. A short distance from Mt Etna in Termina had beauty and life. Mt Etna had its signs of destruction that had come and gone. The lake of fire John describes is a never-ending death. The Book of Enoch, written by a biblical figure who lived before the Great Flood, depicts this same picture. It contains apocalyptic visions, ethical teachings, and descriptions of heavenly realms and divine judgments. The Books of Enoch, although not part of the canonical scriptures, significantly influence Jewish and Christian theology. Enoch contains vivid descriptions of fierce places of punishment. Here is one:

Those days they shall be led off to the abyss of fire and to the torment and the prison in which they shall be confined forever.
Then Semjaza [one of the leaders of the fallen angels] shall be burnt up with the condemned, and they will be destroyed, having been bound together with them
to the end of all generations.
(1 Enoch 10:13-14)

After John's tortuous scene, we have our text, "Then I saw a great White Throne and Him who sat on it, from whose face the earth and the heaven fled away. And there was found no place for them" (Rev. 20:11). The scene we have is all people before Christ. That means rich and poor, rulers and the ruled, famous and non-famous, all brought before the throne. The sea gave up those who died, declaring there was no place untouched by this judgment. Adam and Eve tried to hide. John declares that the depths of the seas cannot hide dead souls. The dead will arise and find themselves at this great judgment. There was no escaping what was about to happen. We can be assured that none of them willingly came here. They never figured they would have to give an account of their life. The very mockers in Peter's day are here. No one escapes. Unbelievers convince themselves that all suffering ends at death. Death is the liberator of pain. If, by some chance, death is not the end, they are good enough to make it to heaven or whatever they want to call it.

We all heard comments, "I will have company in hell." There is no company. There is the utmost loneliness that a person cannot even imagine. The Great White Throne Judgment describes what happens. The phrase, "Him who sat on it, from whose face the earth and the heaven fled away. An there was found no place for them" (Rev. 20:11) suggests the overwhelming presence and power of God, before whom even the elements of creation seem to vanish or flee. This imagery emphasized the awe-inspiring nature of God's judgment and the absolute authority He holds over all creation. It tells us a day of reckoning is happening, and all people will stand before Him and give an account of their lives. The idea is there is no place for them to escape or hide. There are no appeals. This judgment is the final and absolute judge to whom everyone must give account. The imagery reminds us of the first judgment in the garden, where Adam and Eve tried to hide. King David's life experiences would have reminded him that there was no escaping the watchful eye of God.

> Where can I go from Your Spirit?
> Or where can I flee from Your presence?
> If I ascend into heaven, You are there;
> If I make my bed in hell [Sheol], behold, You are there.
> If I take the wings of the morning,
> And dwell in the uttermost parts of the sea...
> Even the night shall be light about me;
> Indeed, the darkness shall not hide from You.
> (Ps. 139:7-12)

The Books are Opened

We all can remember playing hide and seek as children. It was even more challenging when we played the game when darkness crept upon us. John tells us there is no place to hide from God. The scene depicts the tension in introducing the two books. You can almost feel the nervousness in the imagery that John uses. "The books were opened" (Rev.

20:12). The opening heightens the tension, leaving us wondering if those there know the outcome. There were two books: the Book of Works and the Book of Life. Let us examine the second book first: The Book of Life. One commentator writes, "The first book opened will probably be the Scriptures, the Word of God which contains the revelation of God's holy character, the moral law, the declaration of humanity's sinfulness and God's plan of salvation by faith in the Savior. This book also reveals that even when men do not have the written Word, they have the law of God written in their hearts (Rom. 2:14-16) and the revelation of God's consciousness in creation (Rom. 1:20; 2:12). All men are responsible for the revelation they have and stand at this judgment because of their own negative volition to God's grace (Rom. 1:18; 2:4, 14; John 7:17). So then, Scripture will show the clearness of the plan of God and that man is without excuse."[15] It is also possible that the ungodly before a holy God, their sinfulness will be evident to them. Perhaps no words will need to be said because God has written on the hearts of humanity that He exists. Whatever happens, they will know what the Book of Life means, and their name is nowhere to be found. Their name not found determines their fate. Each one's panic would be too horrible to grasp as they try to understand the Book of Life.

Our first encounter with the Book of Life is when the Israelites make the golden calf, and Moses pleads with God to spare them. (Ex. 32:32-33). It also appears in Psalms 69:28, Daniel 4:3, and Philippians 4:3. The Tree of Life and the Book of Life have a close connection. The Tree of Life, first introduced to us in Genesis, symbolizes eternal life. God had prevented Adam and Eve from eating from the Tree of Life. They would have lived in their fallen state for eternity, destined for doom. The Boof of Life determines what and where your life will be. Revelation 2:7, 22:2, 14, 19 promises access to life in the New Jerusalem.

We can see the symbolism as the Book of Life lifted high so everyone can see if their name is there. I recall taking a twelve-week tractor-trailer course. At the end of the course, an instructor assessed my driving skills. Later that day, I ran to the board to check if I qualified. I can only imagine the tension in this judgment. Only the names of those who accepted Christ's name are there. It is He who took their place on the cross. It is He whom believers declare their righteousness. The panic on the faces of the ungodly must be unbearable as the reality finally takes hold, knowing the fate that awaits them. Adam and Eve pointed fingers at each other, trying to pass the blame. At this judgment, pointing fingers and passing blame is an automated response, as they try to pass their responsibility onto another. You can almost hear the excuses.

My parents never took me to Sunday School, so I didn't get the chance to hear about You, Jesus.

Mom and Dad never gave me the Opportunity. It's their fault my name is not there—Jesus! It is my school, college's fault. They taught me things against you. I listened to the government and the media; I didn't have a chance. It is those books I read. They will continue to make excuse after excuse, and nothing will change. They have sealed their fate by rejecting Christ. Salvation was a gift, and they rejected it. They will understand when the judge says, "I took the place on the *CROSS* for Christians, and I then judged their works. They are righteous because I am righteous. You're judged for who you are and are standing on your own righteous. "The judge declares I measure you by my holiness and deem you unholy. I can almost hear the whys. Why did I listen when _____ tried to tell me about Jesus? Why did I think it was all hogwash? The question "Why?" haunts them for eternity.

Interestingly, a few chapters back mention the Lamb's Book of Life (Rev. 13)—John's vision emphasizes that the Lamb has now risen and stands as a judge. John does not want anyone to forget the most essential fact. Only those names in the Lamb's Book of Life are in the new glorious city. Only those who Christ died and bled for.

Now, let us examine the first book, The Book of Works. The Book of Works records every action, selfish thought, and every deed, good or bad. Because God has written his law on everyone's heart, even unbelievers do good deeds. God judges every unbeliever based on their knowledge and every opportunity they have had to do good. "Can you imagine the massive sinking feeling that will sweep across the vast multitude of the godless when they see the Lord open the book of the Ten Commandments? These commandments present how God expected them, his creatures and the recipients of his countless blessings, to live. The first commandment required them to have no other god, and what a terrifying thing it would be to stand there in his presence with full, piercing knowledge of all the things they have put before God—material things, pleasure, sexual immorality and careers."[16] The judge proceeds through each commandment and says you used my name as it meant nothing. You cursed and spoke of me in the most vile manner. They faced the judge and were found guilty. Why discuss works when the Book of Life has already determined their fate, you may ask? Their works will decide their punishment in the Lake of Fire.

Jesus condemns the towns of Chorazin, Bethsaida, and Capernaum for witnessing His miracles, hearing the gospel, and then rejecting Him. Jesus said it would be more tolerable for Sodom and Gomorrah on the day of judgment than for them (Matt. 11-23-24 and LK. 10:12-15). Dr. Lutzer writes, "They will be judged on the basis of what they did with what they knew, or should have known; thus, hell will not be the same for everyone."[17] We may have heard someone say sin is sin. That is true, but not all sins are equal. Yes, all are sinners who fall short of the glory of God (Rom. 3:23). Some sins are more grievous because of their nature and the harm they cause. Jesus speaks to Pontius Pilate, who presides over His trial, and said, "You could have no power at all against Me unless it had been given you from above. Therefore the one who delivered Me to you has the greater sin" (Jn. 19:11). The apostle James writing a warning of the seriousness of what is taught, "My brethren, let not many of you become teachers, knowing that we shall receive a stricter judgment" (3:1). Listen to what Jesus says, to those who hear, and know but continue to sin, "And the servant who knows his master's will, and did not prepare himself or do according to his will, shall be beaten with many stripes. But he who did not know, yet committed things deserving of stripes, shall be beaten with few. For everyone to whom much is given, from him much will be required; and to whom much has been committed, of him they will ask the more" (LK. 12:47-48). The Hitler's will receive greater punishment. Every person will have their judgment determined by the righteous judge before Him. The righteous judge will carefully review every deed done and not done, action or inaction, and influence you could have had and had. Jesus says it would have been better if Judas was not born (Matt. 26:24).

The apostle Paul says, "But because you are stubborn and refuse to turn from your sin, you are storing up terrible punishment for yourself. For a day of anger is coming, when God's righteous judgment will be revealed. He will judge everyone according to what they have done. He will give eternal life to those who keep on doing good, seeking after the glory and honor and immortality that God offers. But he will pour out his anger and wrath on those who live for themselves, who refuse to obey the truth and instead live lives of wickedness" (Rom.2:5-8, NLT).

Every good thing comes from God. Matthew's gospel points out that the rain falls on all, both the just and the unjust (5:45). James says every perfect gift comes from above (1:17). Therefore, talents or abilities do not matter what you call them; they come from God. Therefore, the individual is accountable for that ability. All role models are responsible for what they are demonstrating. God will consider what you did with that talent and your message. He will consider your giving, your helping. Just as Christians are accountable for their gifts and opportunities and will receive or lose rewards, the unbelievers are also under examination, and their actions will determine their punishment. Jesus said as much as you have done to them, you have done unto Me (Matt. 25:1-46). Do not think because a person can buy their way by giving a large sum or having a hospital wing built in their name. The all-knowing God will expose selfish motives, and nothing will evade His sight.

He will take everything into account in His passing punishment. Is there an actual fire?

My response is the language and imagery depict the most horrible experience possible. Loneliness, depression, anger, the most extreme feeling possible is what John is trying to describe. When God is absent, all goodness disappears, and words become incapable of describing it. No words can fully describe the fate that awaits those who rejected Christ and are determined to go on their own. Just before the final sentencing and after they realize all their excuses fail, their true nature takes over, and they curse God. We know this because Revelation 16 describes a time of tribulation when humanity will experience great suffering. And people curse God for what is happening (16:11). It is plausible to assume that some individuals might react similarly during this judgment. With their hardened hearts and the removal of God's presence, evil takes over. Chapter 20:15 ends in horrifying. It is so frightening. It is heart-wrenching to write the words, so I am leaving it for you to read. Just as horrifying chapter 20 ends, chapter 21 begins with a new beginning, "Now I saw a new heaven and a new earth, for the first heaven earth had passed away. Also, there is no sea." No more chaos. No more pain.

Heavenly Father,
we bow our heads before You in Jesus' name.
I confess it was difficult to look at the White

Throne Judgment.
It isn't easy to discuss, but it is necessary.
May we see the seriousness of rejecting Jesus.
Father, I ask You to quicken our hearts so that
more people will desire the gift of life You offer.
With open hearts, we confess with our mouths that
You, Jesus, died for us.
In You, Jesus, we have life.
In Jesus' name, Amen.

---

[1] Roop, Eugene, F., Believers Church Bible Commentary, Genesis, Herald Press, Scottdale, Pennsylvania, Kitchener, Ontario, 1987, P. 83.

[2] Alcorn, Randy, P. 244.

[3] Marshall, Paul; Gilbert, Lela, P. 239.

[4] Marshall, Pau; Gilbert, Lela, P. 32-33.

[5] Yeatts, John R., Believers Church Bible Commentary, Revelation, Hearld Press Scottdale, Pennsylvania Waterloo, Ontario, 1946, P. 401.

[6] Wilson, William, Old Testament Word Studies, Kregel Publications Grand Rapids, Michigan, 1978, P. 373.

[7] Marshall, Paul; Gilbert, Lela, P. 86.

[8] Larson, Craig, Brain; Ene Elshof, P. 234

[9] Vine, W. E.; Unger Merrill F.; White, Willian Jr., An Expository Dictionary of Biblical Words, Thomas Nelson Publisher, Nashville, Camden, New York, 1985, P. 337.

[10] Lutzer, Erwin W. Your Eternal Reward, Moody Publisher 820 N. LaSalle Boulevard Chicago, IL 60610, 2015, P. 149.

[11] Alcorn, Randy, P. 602-603.

[12] Garrett, James Leo Jr., Systematic Theology Bible, Historical, and Evangelical Vol 2 2nd, Wiff & stock, Eugene, Oregon, 2014, P. 863.

[13] Larson, Craig Brian; Ten Elshof, Phyllis, P. 435.

[14] Larson, Craig Brian; Ten Elshof, Phyllis, P.415.

[15] Hamption, J Keathley III, Studies in Revelation, Lesson 29: The Reign of Christ and the Great White Throne (20:11-15), The Books, Biblical Studies Press, 2007.

[16] Ellsworth, Roger, Opening up Revelation, Day One Publication, 2013, P. 137-138.

[17] Lutzer, Erwin W., P. 158.

Chapter Six
Now What?

Ask, and it will be given to you; seek, and
and you will find; knock, and it will be
opened to you. For everyone who ask receives,
and he who seeks finds, and to him who knocks
it will be opened. Or what man is there among
you who, if his son asks for bread, will give him
a stone? Or if he asks for a fish, will he give him
a serpent? If you then, being evil, know how to
give good gifts to your children, how much more
will your Father who is in heaven give good
things to those who ask Him! Therefore, whatever
you want men to do to you, do also to them, for
this is the law and the prophets. Enter by the
narrow gate; for wide is the gate and broad is the
way that leads to destruction, and there are many
who go in by it. Because narrow is the gate and
difficult is the way which leads to life, and there
are few who find it. (Matt. 7:7-14).

As we approach the end of our journey, I will conclude by emphasizing what we discussed and aiming to guide our paths toward hope. Hope is a deliberate choice, and that choice is Jesus. Let me begin with a story.

I can recall the day, December 29[th,] 2009. It was a Tuesday evening; not just any Tuesday; this Tuesday was going to change lives forever. My daughter and I walked down the corridor of the Dartmouth General Hospital. It was a day that would leave an imprint on the lives of two vital people to me. What was I going to say? What was I going to do? As we walked through the corridor, I could hear no sound other than words shouting in my head. If my daughter spoke, I did not hear her, over the words racing through my mind. They were so loud I thought my head would explode. Why? The strange thing about words is that when you mix them with feelings, they may not make sense. If I could have run away, I would have. We entered the room, and she lay there, lifeless. No sound or stirring came. I felt overwhelmed with memories. There are memories I wish I didn't have.

Memories of burying a child who lived ten hours. Memories of saying things I wished I had never said. I wanted to speak a word of comfort - anything but no word came. Tears filled my eyes, and a lump filled my throat; it was so big that no words could come from my lips. My daughter sat beside her mom, and I stood there helpless. God was nowhere to be found in my head, which seemed strange coming from a former pastor. I had walked down corridors of hospitals many times before. It was not as if I had not sat at the bedside of a dying person before, but this was different—this was the mother of my children. I knew she would look forward to meeting Jesus. Please understand me. If she had had a choice, she would have stayed. Death takes the choice out of our hands. Sandra died that night. She is in peace and comfort in the arms of Jesus. The lives left behind had hurt, guilt, and many other feelings to face. Those feelings leave a lasting imprint and a lasting imprint they left.

You may recall that I mentioned that the apostle Paul looked forward to being with Jesus, but facing one's death differs from facing the death of a loved one. Paul was grieving when his friend Epaphroditus was sick. He said that if something happened to his dear friend, he would "have sorrow upon sorrow" (Phil. 2:27). I mention this because we live in a world of sorrow and pain, which can often be unfair. The apostle Paul tells us that Christ has taken the sting out of death, but he would never want us to think there is no pain (1 Cor. 15:55-58). There may be times when we feel God has abandoned us.

Remember, they are feelings and have nothing to do with the truth. God is there if we feel Him or not. There may come a time when you cry, throw up your hands, and say this makes no sense. Why

Jesus? But those cries tell us we not only want Jesus, we need Him, but that He is God. It is then we need to cry unto Him for comfort. It is then we discover only He can help. As King David was in sorrow, he said when he lost his son, he could not come to me, but I will go to him (2 Sam. 12:23). Paul says that is our hope. That is the promise of the CROSS.

That road is not always a simple journey; questions under challenging times often make us struggle more. Does Sandra know she has four beautiful grandchildren? Dr. Randy Alcorn says Christians know. Two texts serve as the basis for his argument. 1 Samuel 28 tells the story of King Saul falling out of favor with God. He was going to be facing the Philistines, and he was afraid. He became desperate. I am unsure if you have ever felt that way, but it is a feeling of panic, and you become overwhelmed and helpless. You may grab anything if it could take away what you feel. Saul was desperate. He wanted advice and guidance, so he disguised himself and sought a medium called the Witch of Endor. The medium was hesitant because it was unlawful to be a medium, but she proceeded, and to her surprise, Samuel, the prophet's spirit, appeared. Samuel knew what was happening with Saul and told him that the Philistines would defeat Israel because of his disobedience. Because Samuel knew he must have seen. The other text Dr. Alcorn uses is Revelation 6, where the martyrs cry, "How long, O Lord, holy and true until You judge and avenge our blood on those who dwell on the earth?" He says the martyrs must know what is happening and asks God how long it will be before the judgment. Dr. Alcorn says God could have allowed Samuel and the martyrs to see what was happening. He also recognizes that what they see does not mean it is a common occurrence—he does believe that is the reality for those in heaven. I do not know if it is a common occurrence, and there are insufficient scripture references to base that argument. We do not have all the answers to those mysterious questions, but we can fully trust God, and whatever we may lose in this life, God will more than make up for it in His new creation. Scripture tells us He loves to give. Jesus on the mount, looking down over the multitude, says, "So if you sinful people know how to give good gifts to your children, how much more will your heavenly Father give good gifts to those who ask him" (Matt. 7:11, NLT). Jesus wanted them and us to know that no one can out-give God.

The text in which this final chapter, Matthew 7, begins refers to the Sermon on the Mount. Jesus stands on a mount overlooking Galilee and gives the last of His ethical and moral teachings. He tells the listeners you provide good gifts to your children. Your heavenly Father gives more. What Jesus is saying is that you who are sinful and living in a wicked world want to give gifts to your children, but how much more the holy God wants to give? (v. 11).

Jesus says what you need to do is ask. What Jesus tells them they need to ask for is wisdom. Wisdom on how to live in this sinful world. Why, the road is hard. Jesus calls it a narrow road to life (v. 14). How relevant it is for our society. Living in a culture where right is wrong and wrong is right. Media is not journalism but indoctrination (v. 14-15). Schools and colleges can be centers of indoctrination. The world wants us to believe what they believe, which can often be an unchristian worldview. Yes, the media is determined not only by political and corporate decisions but also by profit. Do they not give what they believe their viewer wants? What society wants sadly reflects its fallen state. Jesus says you will know them by their fruits. Does their way lead to life or death? (v. 16-17).

Jesus says you need wisdom. Many things will pull you away from the faith. You are going to need wisdom in making judgments. We need wisdom when we look at others. Look at yourself first, recognize your failures and your sinfulness, and in doing so, you will respond compassionately (v. 5). In this text, we have the famous golden rule: do unto others as you would have them do to you. (v. 12). Jesus says not everyone you encounter will be suitable, even those who say they follow me. (v. 21). Jesus hints at the coming judgment when He says everyone will not be a part of my kingdom. (v. 21-23). He emphasizes the need for wisdom when discussing building on a lasting foundation (v. 24-27).

Jesus comes down from the mountain and continues His ministry of healing and teaching, and in chapter 8, we have a clear picture of what will happen to the ungodly. (v. 12). Sadly, the chapter ends with the entire city wanting nothing to do with Jesus and telling Him to leave. Not only do they ask Jesus to go, but they beg Him to leave (v. 34). What does Jesus do? "So He got into a boat, crossed over, and came to His city." (Matt. 9:1). The city had determined their fate. Jesus gave them what they wanted. He turned His back and left. Jesus wanted his followers to know their kingdom was not this world. This world was not their home. Our path may be an arduous journey. Our hope is Heaven. C.S. Lewis says, "Aim at Heaven and you will get earth thrown in: aim at earth and you will get neither."[1] We must set our focus on truth. Jesus is the Truth and the Way (Jn. 14:6).

Heaven is our home, and we can understand why Jesus said, I go to prepare a place for you. If Jesus had returned 500 years ago, the home he would have prepared would have differed dramatically from the one He will prepare. That may sound like a strange comment. When God creates the new heaven and earth, they are one. John illustrates this in what he sees as heaven coming down (Rev. 21:1-2). The new earth will be like the Garden of Eden but will also differ. The new earth will have advancements: new structures, different opportunities, and a place where we will work, grow, and continue to advance. We will continually grow in knowledge and awareness of God. There will be glorious cities—John describes one. The world will be perfect, like the first creation. There will be harmony between humanity and its creation, like the first. In the first creation, humanity grew in knowledge. We remove sin from whom we now are, and our growth in knowledge will continue to expand. It will expand for good. Well, we know everything, of course not. We will not be gods.

It would be fantastic when our bodies resembled Jesus' resurrected body. Jesus passed through closed doors. The apostle Paul says, "Who will transform our lowly body that it may be conformed to His glorious body, according to the working by which He is able even to subdue all things to Himself" (Phil. 3:21). And the apostle John says, "Beloved, now we are children of God; and it has not yet been revealed what we shall be, but we know that when He is revealed, we shall be like Him, for we shall see Him as He is" (1 Jn. 3:2). There is a great mystery of what we will be capable of. I love to let my imagination dream and see me floating above the waters and mountains. Now I said I love to let my imagination dream—That is what it is because heaven remains a mystery. Like Jesus told the listeners on the Mountain, the heavenly Father loves to give marvelous gifts. I cannot even imagine the rewards Jesus may hand out. Listen to what the Apostle Paul tells the Church in Ephesus: "Now to Him who is able to do exceedingly abundantly above all that we ask or think, according to the power that works in us, in Him be glory in the Church by Christ Jesus to all generations, forever and ever Amen." (Eph. 3:20-21). When you let your heart and mind dwell upon what Paul tells the Church, perhaps our imagination is not big enough to see what Christ has in store for us. What are we? Followers of the way - Jesus' way. The epistle to the Hebrews tells us we are people of faith. "Now faith is the assurance of things hoped for, the conviction of things not seen" (Heb. 11:1, ESV).

Contrary to the old saying, being so heavenly-minded that you are no earthly good is untrue. If we look at the many monumental architectures and paintings, they were all heavenly-minded. The Sistine Chapel was commissioned by Pope Julius II and painted by Michelangelo in 1508 at 33; he lay on his back for hours and was finished four years later. The Notre Dame de Paris France - this Gothic cathedral, begun in 1163 and completed in 1345, is renowned for its architectural innovations and its role as a spiritual center. With our technology, we could have created it in less time. Perhaps today, we are not heavenly-minded enough. Our focus is on quickly building buildings mainly for necessity and profits.

Power, greed, and war follow the way of humanity. We do not design such beautiful primary pieces. It is not profitable. Humanity's heart is not towards heaven but earthbound, thinking they can make heaven on earth. That is why scripture says to fill our minds with God's word. Proverbs says, "For as he thinks in his heart, so is he" (23:7). We perhaps do not understand the depth of those words. People who gulf themselves in hate speech, destruction, or any other decisive words will affect them. We know if we fill our bodies with junk food, our bodies will break down. Why do we not think that we will do anything less if we fill our minds with that which causes improper behavior? What is in our minds will lead to our actions. Scripture encourages us to dwell on those things that build us up. "And now, dear brothers and sisters, one final thing. Fix your thoughts on what is true, and honorable, and right, and pure, and lovely, and admirable. Think about things that are excellent and worthy of praise. Keep putting into practice all you learned and received from me—everything you heard from me and saw me doing. Then the God of peace will be with you" (Phil. 4:8-9, NLT).

Christ promises us something better. Jesus is preparing us for a home and a home where we will work, learn, laugh, hike, walk through the perfect field, and enjoy relationships. Our minds cannot imagine what awaits us if we make Jesus our Lord. "IF "is a tiny word but can have profound implications. It is a decision only you can make. It matters not the color of your skin, your education, or the money in your bank. Christ is the righteous judge. The apostle Paul writes to the Roman Church: "In fact, it says, The message is very close at hand; it is on your lips and in your heart. And that message is the very message about faith that we preach: If you openly declare that Jesus is Lord and believe in your heart that God raised him from the dead, you will be saved" (Rom.10:8-9). What we are declaring is that we are a sinner separated from God. Christ died for us, and when He rose from the grave, He promised us Life.

This new creation God will create for us will be a beautiful and exciting place to spend eternity. J. C. Ryle says, "Let us not be afraid to meditate often on the subject of heaven, and to rejoice in the prospect of good things to come. Indeed, let us take comfort in the remembrance of the other side. We ought to look to look up and look forward! The time is short. The world is growing old. The coming of the Lord draweth nigh."[2] You have a choice before you. My family has heard me say, I will leave this earth when my Lord declares my time is up. Listen to just a few of them:

1. "You [God] have decided the length of our lives. You know how many months we will live, and we are not given a minute longer." (Job 14:5, NLT).

2. "You [God] saw me before I was born. Every day of my life was recorded in your book. Every moment was laid out before a single day had passed. (Ps. 139:16, NLT).
3. "The Lord makes firm the steps of those who delights in him." (Ps. 37:23, NLT).

The marvelous thing about My God is that His word tells me He is in charge of my life and the world. Sometimes, He gives nations what they deserve; other times, He rises and tears down, all to bring about His purpose. "Blessed be the name of God forever and ever, For wisdom and might are His. And He changes the times and the seasons; He removes kings and raises up kings; He gives wisdom to the wise And knowledge to those who have understanding" (Dan. 2:20-21). Despite humanity's chaos, greed, power struggles, and need to control, He will accomplish His purpose.

You know God is real. We know there is a heaven. Listen to what people say after they lose a loved one. "I know they are watching me." "I hope they are proud of me." Their very being is a cry of the heart to be reconnected from that which sin separated. We who believe know there is a personal God. I know Jesus has gone to prepare a place for me. I pray He is preparing a place for you.

Perhaps now is vital to deal with an important question. If you are anything like me, you may say, are you not relying on the Bible for your arguments? With its many translations, how can we trust it? This book's purpose is not to prove the Bible. There are many books written on the reliability of scriptures. I will mention a couple of books if you want to look further into that subject:

1. "Is the Bible Reliable?" by Focus on the Family. The author gears this book towards a broader audience, including those new to biblical reliability.
2. "The New Evidence That Demands a Verdict," by Josh McDowell. This book is more comprehensive and detailed, providing substantial evidence, historical data, and arguments supporting the reliability of Scripture.

Dr. Voddie Baucham makes a brief argument for the reliability of scriptures, which I believe will help enhance our reassurance of God's word. He derives his argument from the scriptures, 1 Peter 1:16-21, 1 John 1:1-3, and 1 Corinthians 15 are but a few. Right now, you may say that is circular reasoning, using something to prove itself, not really. There are over 25000 archaeological digs that confirm the Bible. There are over 6000 manuscripts of the New Testament from the 1st, 2nd, and centuries. We have early translations into Greek, Syriac, Coptic, and Latin. Historical figures like Homer, Julius Caesar, and Socrates have far fewer manuscripts. There are more manuscripts of the New Testament than any other ancient figure. If we cannot believe in the reliability of the New Testament, we cannot trust any other antiquities documents, which have far less evidence. Someone may say I am a person of science, but remember, the scientific method means three things: something must be observable, measurable, and repeatable. That, of course, would remove all of history. Dr. Baucham gives this definition for belief in the Bible, "It is a reliable collection of historical documents written by eyewitnesses during the lifetime of other eyewitnesses, and they report supernatural events that took place in fulfillment of specific prophecies that proclaim the writing is divine other than human origin." Prophecies like Isaiah 53 and Jesus quote from Psalm 22 on the cross: "My God, My God, why have You forsaken Me?" For further evidence, if all we had were the early church fathers' commentaries on the New Testament, we would have all the New Testament but eleven verses. You can trust God's word. When you hear the pull of the Holy Spirit upon your heart, respond, for doing nothing is your response.

---

[1] Lewis, C.S., Mere Christianity, Musaicum Books, 2017, P. 57.

[2] Rhodes, Ron, The Wonder of Heaven, Havest House Publishing, Eugene, Oregon, 2009, P. 205.

Epilogue:

My view of heaven changed from my junior years of thinking it would be boring, a place you go not because you want but because it is better than the alternative. To a place that would be familiar, exciting, and perfect. How we may see something can shape our response to what we face. Our response to what we face will shape our way of living. How we live will affect not only us but also everything around us. Let me illustrate what I am talking about with a story from when I was a kid and experienced a snowstorm. As a kid, I can recall living in rural Nova Scotia, where fierce snowstorms would occur. This snowstorm was so big we thought it would reach the pole lines. The grownups saw power outages and road and business closures as difficulties, which was true for them. We kids saw snow tunnels, forts, and snowball fights as adventures. We saw what would be when we were let loose to put our imagination to work. Understand me, I am not saying heaven is just a matter of using one imagination. I am saying it is a world perspective — A Christian world perspective.

In my Dream Big journal, I wrote about Justin Brierley's interview with Dr. John Lennox. During the interview, Brierley asked Lennox about one of his most memorable debates. He momently paused and, with a smile, said it was with Dr. Peter Singer. Dr. Singer, an Australian moral philosopher, gained recognition for his bioethics and animal rights work. Dr. Lennox tells Brierley he had begun his debate with Peter Singer by saying his parents were Christians. Dr. Singer quickly states that people tend to remain in the faith they were raised in. Dr. Lennox politely asked Dr. Singer, what are your parents? Dr. Singer replies Atheists. Dr. Lennox said you stayed in the faith in which you grew up. Dr. Singer sharply responds. But it isn't a faith. Dr. Lennox smiled and said, "Peter, I thought you believed it?" Everyone has a worldview, even if they do not realize it.

The Christian worldview is as follows:

1. Christians believe in One God who is eternal, omnipotent, and omniscient. God, the creator and sustainer of everything, loves His creation. He has a purpose and order for humanity; He made us stewards of His creation.

2. God creates humans in His image, giving each person inherent dignity and worth. Humanity was disobedient and chose its own way to live apart from Him. By doing so, humanity fell from grace and needs redemption. Humanity does not even know something is missing. It is like a fish in water, which does not know it's in water until it is out of water.

3. Jesus came as a gift from God, offering us hope. Through faith, we understand we are reconnecting with our true purpose.
4. Christians believe in absolute moral truths. These truths guide us in how we live. Through the power of the Holy Spirit, God's word guides and instructs us on how to live. Morals and ethics are not changeable but are signs of humanity's lostness. We do not preach morals; we preach Christ crucified.
5. Jesus is patient and wants all to experience His new creation. His new creation will be a place to work, grow, laugh, and live fully with our king.

As a Christian, it does not mean we will suffer less. Jesus tells His followers they will suffer more. His followers will face misunderstanding, hatred, mockery, and condemnation. Why? It is a fight against darkness, against that which is untrue. Jesus encourages Christians to keep their faith. Throughout history, persecution fueled the church's growth, and when nations were blessed, apathy eventually took hold. That explains something about our very nature, which we must always be aware of to keep the faith. The apostle Paul says, "I have fought the good faith, I have finished the race, I have kept the faith. Finally, there is laid up for me the crown of righteousness, which the Lord, the righteous Judge, will give me on that Day, and not to me only, but also to all who have loved His appearing" (2 Tim. 4:7-8).

Dr. John Lennox has had many debates and has given many interviews. Perhaps one of the most important interviews I had the privilege of listening to took place in 2019. The interviewer asked him what his final words of wisdom would be to his children. Dr. Lennox replied, not only to his children but to everybody. He said Christians are robbing themselves of the most essential thing in life, which is to spend time in God's word. Through God's word, we are fellowshipping with God. We will make no impact on the world if we do not spend time in God's word. You cannot do it by reading the Bible 5 minutes before bedtime. He says a husband will have no impact if they are not praying with their wife, and your children must know you are doing this. Christians can rise in their careers but never make time for God's word. I thought about what Dr. Lennox said, and God's word said the same thing. Listen to the writer to the Hebrews, "You have been believers so long now that you ought to be teaching others. Instead, you need someone to teach you again the basic things about God's word. You are like babies who need milk and cannot eat solid food. For someone who lives on milk is still an infant and doesn't know how to do what is right. Solid food is for those who are mature, who through training have the skill to recognize the difference between right and wrong" (Heb. 5:12-14, NLT).

I hear people saying you don't need a church to be a Christian. I didn't get saved in a church building, but you will remain a babe if you believe you can grow in a relationship without fellowship in God's word. There are no isolated Christians in heaven. Satan's job is to keep you away from fellowshipping in God's word. He doesn't want you to worship with others. He wants you to think all is well without reading or hearing God's word. When I walked into Aunt Mabel's hospital room as a babe, God never wanted me to remain a babe.

You do not need to go to seminary to grow in a relationship with God. Spending time in God's word and sitting under the teaching of a Bible-preaching pastor will see your faith flourish. I am privileged to have a profound teacher of God's word in the Church I call home. Being retired has many advantages. It gave me the time to write this, and I benefit, perhaps more than anyone else. But I also benefit from watching my wife get out of bed, get coffee, and spend hours in God's word. I have the privilege of seeing God at work. Developing a relationship with Christians will aid your growth, and there is no better place than a local Bible-believing church.

We must remain strong in the mission that Jesus gave to us. The message is that Christ offers life, and there is no life apart from Him. Before we end this journey, I think it is helpful if we ask ourselves seven questions:

1. What is my purpose in life?

Reflect on what drives you, what you desire in life, and what you want to achieve. That very reflection is your worldview.

2. Is my purpose achievable?

Consider if your goals are realistic and attainable with the resources and abilities you can gain.

3. Even if I achieve my purpose, what does that mean?

"For God will bring every work into judgment, including every secret thing, whether good or evil" (Ecc. 12:14). "For what profit is it to a man if he gains the world and loses his own soul" (Matt. 16:26).

4. Am I prepared for the worst?

Over the past 60 years, many Western societies have seen a decline in Christian values. At the opening of the 2024 Olympics in France, they mocked Christianity. News media told stories of drag queens lining a long table mocking the Last Supper. Europe, which flourished in Christianity and spread to America, seeing blessing upon blessing because of the rise in Christianity, is witnessing a decline. If the Western world considered its history, it would see how it benefited from Christianity. It is demonic what is happening, not considering what Christianity has contributed to society. And it is now turning against that which gave its rise. With the threat of World War III hanging over the world and economic instability, uncertainty seems everywhere; humanity believes it can solve the world's issues apart from God, but we know differently, and history has proved us right.

5. Is there any hope when the worst happens?

Identify your deepest fears or the worst-case scenarios that could happen in your life.

6. What would change if Jesus was my hope?

Would the answer to this question change your response to the other questions?

7. How do I live in an upside-down world?

This question is indeed profound, especially in times of uncertainty. This question becomes more momentous if you are a parent. What do I tell my children about the truth? The future seems uncertain and can be overwhelming.

These seven questions should not instill a negative response.I repeated these seven questions from a Christian worldview and how the answers changed to optimistic hope. Everything about God leads us to a positive way to live. Following His principles will aid us in getting the most out of life. These words of the apostle Paul tell us how to get the most out of life. "Finally, brothers and sisters, whatever is true, whatever is noble, whatever is pure, whatever is lovely, whatever is admirable—if anything is excellent or praiseworthy—think about such things" (Phil. 4:8, NIV).

We are to fill our hearts and minds with that which brings hope and life. Death, although it brings sadness, for the Christian, it means graduation day. Why is it graduation day, you may ask? All those self-doubts, all those self-abuse thoughts, never-ending second questions, all with every fear and every crushing feeling moment, is laid at the feet of Jesus. Today is the beginning of a lifelong journey of living and growing. The Apostle Paul writes to the Corinthian Church, who had all their struggles and misunderstood something astounding: "Now we see things imperfectly, like puzzling reflections in a mirror, but then we will see everything with perfect clarity. All that I know now is partial and incomplete, but then I will know everything completely, just as God now knows me completely." (1 Cor. 13:12, NLT).

Thirty years ago, I left the pastoral ministry with a broken spirit. That broken spirit hindered everything I did. My friend Junior Tidd had a terminal illness. I received word that he would like me to visit him, and I did so on June 11 of this year. August 3rd was his celebration of life. The service was indeed a declaration of a man who lived his faith. If Junior had not sent word that he wanted to see me, I most likely would not have gone to the celebration of life. I would have written to his wife and family my heartfelt sorrow for their loss. I visited Junior. I went to the celebration, and in doing so, I experienced healing my spirit. I thought how strange. As I was driving to see Junior, I prayed for his healing, and I got healed. Did God tell Junior to contact me? I believe He did. I am so thankful he did. Before I close with prayer, let me remind you each person has a choice. A choice no person can make for you.

Joshua has become an older man and wants to encourage the people of Israel before he dies. Israel had wandered in the promised land for 40 years after coming out of Egyptian captivity. He presents them with a choice of serving other gods or Yahweh, the one and True God. Upon entering a land of a different culture, Israel may face the temptation to go along with this new culture. This new culture had many gods and sacrifices. Joshua lived long enough to understand that people can easily succumb to temptation. That is why Israel ended in captivity, to begin with, turning their back on God. Even after being freed from 400 years of captivity, they once again showed disobedience and wandered in the wilderness for forty years. God is loving. Joshua takes a stand and tells the people he and his household will follow Yahweh no matter their choice (Josh. 24). We make choices every day, and perhaps our choices may even become heart-wrenching in the days ahead. The most important decision you will ever make is what you will do with Jesus. The sad part about that decision is that you make it every day, even if you may not realize it.

Heavenly Father, we come to the end of
this Journey. I pray we see it is not the
end. It is the beginning of something far
Glorious, then these words can declare.
Perhaps that is why heaven is a mystery,
no mere words can adequately describe
What you have in store for your children.
Now, Father, give us the power and wisdom
to live the life, you called us to, and may
we continue that until your Son Jesus calls us
home. I thank You, and I know that You
want to draw close to each of us and use us.
Thank you for using Junior; give him a big
hug and smile from me. In Jesus' name, Amen!

Seven Questions Reflected Positively

1. What is my purpose in Life?

My purpose is to fulfill God's unique plan for me, which brings joy, fulfillment, and meaning. (Jeremiah 29:11)

2. Is my purpose achievable?

With God's guidance and strength, my purpose is achievable, and He equips me for every good work. (Philippians 4:13)

3. Even if I achieve my purpose, what does that mean to me?

He guides my footsteps. (Pr. 3:5-6; Ps. 37:23-24; John 10:10)

4. Am I prepared for the Worst?

God is with me in all circumstances, providing strength, comfort, and hope. (Psalm. 23:4) Paul writes, "And we know that all things work together for good to those who love God, to those who are called according to His purpose" (Rom. 8:28).

5. Is there any hope?

In Christ, I have an everlasting hope that surpasses all challenges and difficulties. (Romans 15:13)

6. What changes for me when I believe in Jesus?

Believing in Jesus transforms my life, filling it with purpose, hope, love, and eternal assurance. (2 Corinthians 5:17)

The promise that God can use our current circumstances and resources to bless us and empower us to bless others, reflecting the covenant God made with Abraham, is where your positive outlook stems from: "I will make you into a great nation, and I will bless you; I will bless those you bless you, and whoever curses you I will curse; and all peoples on earth will be blessed through you" (Gen. 12:2-3).

7. How do I live in an upside-down world?

There is only one way to live: to make God's word a part of your life. The creator who used thought and logic in designing the world gave thought, logic, and reason for living in a fallen world. He did this through his word. Therefore, you need to be a part of a church to grow, gain knowledge, and have fellowship. You gain strength and encouragement from the body of Christ. The pastor needs to preach verse by verse, chapter by chapter. This methodical teaching allows for a deep and thorough understanding of Scripture. This approach ensures the Bible's context, meaning, and nuances are fully explored. That does not mean topical studying God's word is not helpful, for it is. Delving into the logic and what often seems a mystery of the Scriptures can offer profound insights into God's nature, His plan for humanity, and the principles governing a faithful life. When you grasp these deeper truths, you're better prepared to navigate the complexities of life, including the challenges of living in an upside-down world. This understanding can offer guidance, comfort, and strength, enabling you to face difficulties confidently. God is personable, and He will walk with you.

www.ingramcontent.com/pod-product-compliance
Lightning Source LLC
Chambersburg PA
CBHW071324120626
46546CB00002B/425